EDGE OF
MORNING

NATIVE VOICES SPEAK
FOR THE BEARS EARS

BEARS EARS BUTTES
PHOTOGRAPH BY
TIM PETERSON

EDGE OF MORNING

MORNING

NATIVE VOICES SPEAK
FOR THE BEARS EARS

EDITED BY
JACQUELINE KEELER

TORREY HOUSE PRESS
Salt Lake City • Torrey

First Torrey House Press Edition, May 2017
Copyright © 2017 by Torrey House Press

Published by Torrey House Press
Salt Lake City, Utah
www.torreyhouse.org

International Standard Book Number: 978-1-937226-71-8
E-book ISBN: 978-1-937226-72-5
Library of Congress Control Number: 2016943304
Cover art by Shonto Begay, "Peaceful Eve" at modernwestfineart.com
Book design by Alisha Anderson

PERMISSIONS

"A Birthday Poem" from *Blue Horses Rush In: Poems and Stories* by Luci Tapahonso. © 1997 Luci Tapahonso. Reprinted by permission of the University of Arizona Press.

"Guidelines for the Treatment of Sacred Objects" and "The Theft Outright" by Heid E. Erdrich from *National Monuments*. © 2008 Heid E. Erdrich. Reprinted by permission of Michigan State University Press.

"Chinle Summer" and "In Memory of Crossing the Columbia" by Elizabeth Woody. Reprinted by permission of Elizabeth Woody.

DETAIL
PHOTOGRAPH BY
TIM PETERSON

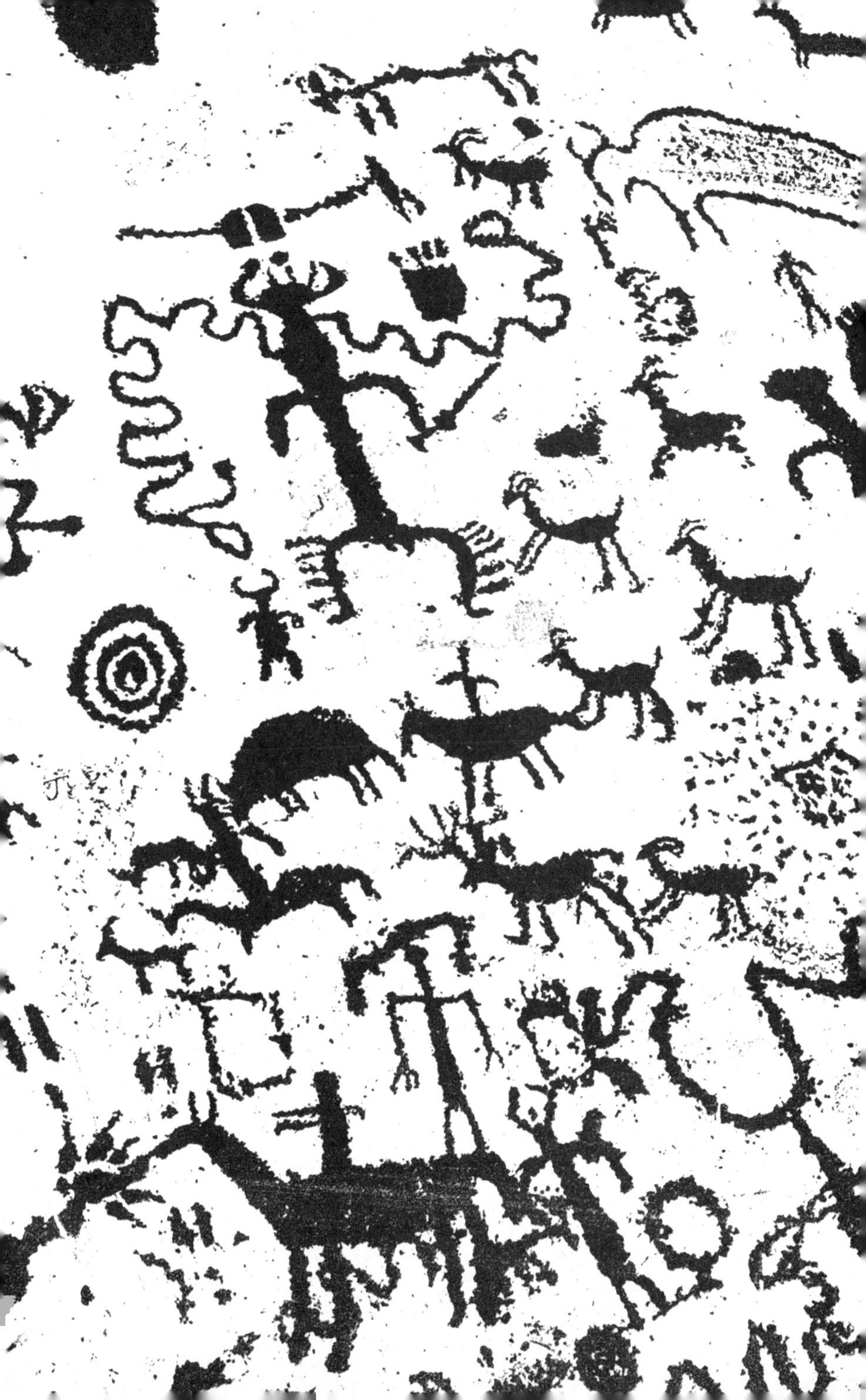

The question has been asked, yet we hear no response: 'What part of sacred don't you understand?' Essentially we're saying why isn't it enough for us to say a site is sacred and should be set aside and protected and respected because it's integral for our spiritual practice to be continued.

— klee benally

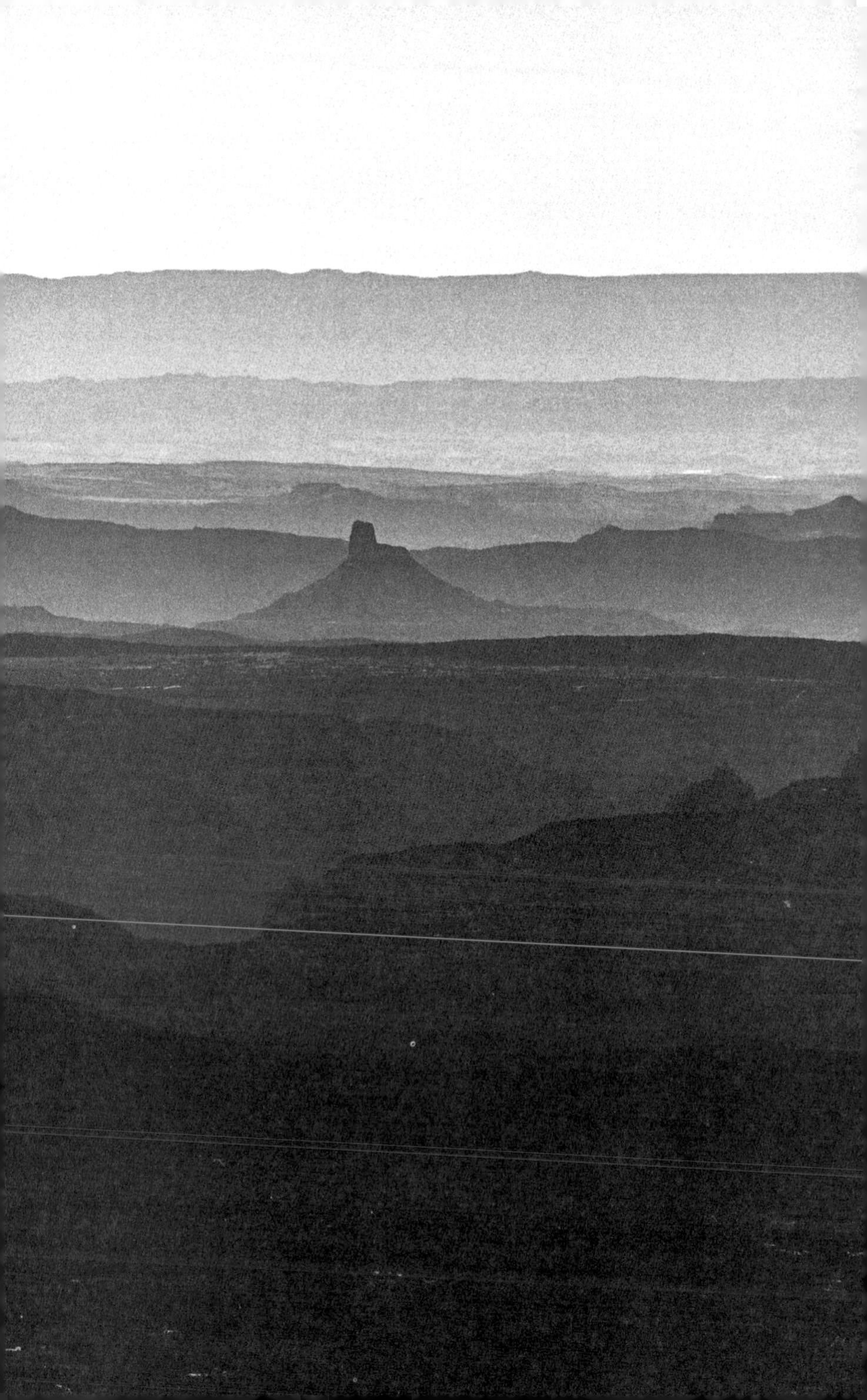

TABLE OF CONTENTS /

ORIGIN STORIES /
Interviews with Bears Ears Inter-Tribal Coalition Organizers

FOR THIS LAND, FOR THE DINÉ BIKÉYAH /
The People's Land Navajo Activists and Academia Speak for Bears Ears

VISTA AT BEARS EARS
PHOTOGRAPH BY TIM PETERSON, FLOWN BY LIGHTHAWK

IN OUR USUAL AND ACCUSTOMED PLACES /
Indigenous Leaders on Bears Ears and the Fight for Cultural
Preservation and Access to Public Lands in the United States

EDGE OF MORNING

MORNING

NATIVE VOICES SPEAK
FOR THE BEARS EARS

INTRODUCTION

JACQUELINE KEELER

IN HER 1944 BOOK *SPEAKING OF INDIANS*, MY GREAT-great aunt Ella Deloria, a Yankton Dakota ethnologist trained under Franz Boas of Columbia University, summarized Dakota/Lakota culture as "a scheme of life that worked." She quoted an elder who urged his children and grandchildren to:

> *Give abundantly and with glorious abandon. Better not to honor someone than dishonor him by doing it haltingly and calculatingly. Pity the coward who gives half holding back, timid for his own private security because he does not put his faith in men but in mere chattel.*

> *My children, it is better to give and have nothing left, if need be, than to appear stingy. Property always flows back in due time to those who let it flow freely forth. In the endless process of giving, that is bound to be so.*

This passage often comes to mind when I think of the fundamental ways in which our traditional societies differed in focus and organizational principles from the colonial system that rules our lives today. In a colonial enterprise, profitability is the measure by which all endeavors and even the people and the land itself, are valued. In Dakota culture, it was our relationships that were the focus and considered the source of wealth, life and, ultimately, true humanity. There were no scenarios in which a person who took only for him or herself would be held in high regard—or even as human—in the Dakota/Lakota society my great-great aunt documented so carefully.

This valuing of relationships extends beyond human beings. Today, Yankton elder and my relative (and Ella's grandniece) Faith Spotted Eagle, whose fight against the Keystone XL and Dakota Access pipelines is discussed in the chapter "Creating a Road Map of Reverence and Sense of Meaning," says,

> *This all goes to our core belief that animals and plants are parts of family units that have intimate relationships with the Earth and so we respect that. We don't have the arrogance to disrupt those relationships. We live in such a different reality than the capitalistic world...America is going to have to hit bottom in order to be able to gain this sense of respect of these intimate relationships that existed on the Earth since time immemorial.*

I posit these two worldviews, indigenous and colonial, and am, as a Diné and Dakota woman living in the twenty-first century, constantly torn between them. There is no way our traditional culture and worldview can persist without being permitted actual space in the physical world to live out these ideas. These cultural values my great-great aunt records cannot merely be intellectual concepts, they must be lived. And yet, our homelands and cultural and sacred spaces are constantly being taken and reallocated for money-making ventures with no regard for toxic outcomes and necessary clean-up or of our lived histories on the land.

In my interview ("Bears Ears and Inter-Tribal Consensus: Fighting for the Land & Building Healing From Within") with Ute tribal leader Regina Lopez-Whiteskunk, she draws these connections directly to the Bears Ears in southeastern Utah:

I'm going to speak specifically to the Bears Ears area—especially the buttes. We always have a focal point and it starts at the center, and I think things radiate out from the center of energy. We have to make sure that heals and it has the opportunity to heal and to be available down the road...

Even today, you know every time I hear something new and great like a new bean species or something that they learn to grow during the great drought—we wouldn't know that if it gets all destroyed or gets piled in a pile of rubbish that one of the oil and gas industries pile over to the side and call it reclamation. It takes a page out of our history.

As I write this introduction, we face a new administration in the White House, the age of Trump with Republican House and Senate who ran on a party platform calling for Congress to pass legislation to "convey certain federally controlled public lands to the states." This language echoes of Ammon Bundy in his takeover of the Malheur Wildlife Refuge in Oregon in January of 2016.

When Ammon's brother Ryan Bundy was questioned about the rights of the Burns Paiute tribe to the wildlife refuge, which was part of their reservation prior to the Bannock Wars, he said, "We also recognize that the Native Americans had the claim to the land, but they lost that claim. There are things to learn from cultures of the past, but the current culture is the most important."

It is noteworthy he regards as the "current culture" one epitomized by cowboys and ranching, which comprises a tiny minority of Americans today. And only 2.7% of those ranchers control 50% of leases on public lands. These include billionaires like the Koch brothers, the Hilton family, and a Hewlett-Packard heiress. And neither Ryan nor Ammon Bundy are themselves ranchers; when I interviewed actual ranchers around Malheur (I covered the story as a journalist) they called them "lost souls." The ranchers and the tribe and the refuge had worked for ten years to create a management compact they were all proud of, and wanted the media to write about it. It failed, however, to catch the interest of the national media and the Bundy's mischaracterization rules much of the public's imagination to this day.

The displacement of our traditional lifeways and connection to the land has terrible consequences. In my interview ("Bears Ears: Bringing the Youth Back to the Reality of the Natural World") with Navajo elder and Utah Diné Bikéyah chairman Willie Grey-eyes, he notes,

> *I think a lot about human relationships to the land. Right now, there is what they call economic-driven concepts. Everybody wants to say, "I have a goal to make a million dollars." That's all there is, people trying to get to heaven on a pile of money. They don't see themselves and are keeping up with the Begays or Yazzies [common Navajo surnames].*

> *Those are some of the developments and learned behavior that is destroying the stability of our families, community and our [Navajo] nation. Then again, what also comes into play is making a fast buck—money. These are the types of behaviors that are being seen on the Navajo Nation and what we are seeking to do with the Bears Ears National Monument is to stabilize our community and to bring the youth back to the reality of the natural world.*

One might ask if jobs are the answer, especially given the push for energy development from the politicians opposed to national monument designation for the Bears Ears. But jobs must be more than short-term, and since our communities are based on the land and not going anywhere, mitigation of industrial damage must be complete.

Today around the Navajo Nation, there are more than five hundred documented open uranium mines that have not yet been cleaned up. Clean-up costs will run into the billions of dollars. And many of these are in traditional communities where the language and the culture are alive and still stand a chance of being passed down to the next generation. So far, the US government and the companies that created the mess—many now long gone and dissolved—have invested little money in effective mitigation. So, another generation of young Navajos grows up exposed to dangerous levels of radiation. Navajo parents are faced with exposing their children to very real health risks when they choose to raise them in these communities near their grandparents where the culture can be passed down.

This is cultural genocide. Is Navajo culture worth the billions it would cost to clean up these mines? Is there the political will in the American government to make it happen? I believe, history has shown us, the answer is no.

And yet, we persevere. We know there is truth in our relationship to the land and that relationship tells us things that we cannot yet forswear. As Navajo elder Jonah Yellowman of Utah Diné Bikéyah says in his interview ("To Take Care of It, To Look After It: Getting Healed by Healing the Land"),

We're here to take care of it. We're here to look after it. We're

here to preserve it, and our medicine people, when they go and get something for a ceremony, they go over there and they'll talk to the plant or whatever they are going to use. If they are going to cut it, they always put corn pollen on it. They put it back together. Wherever they dig around they smooth it out and leave it like the way it is and they walk away from it. We just don't dig it out and make a big hole and just leave it. We don't do that. So, that's who we are as a Native American Indian people. That's who we are. We are here to take care of and look after it. If you take care of it and look after it, it's going to take care of you. You're going to get healed from it and you're going to heal the land, too, like that.

This book is a documentation of how Native people continue to persevere in this fight for the land and our culture. It is in our DNA; we cannot shake it. It is the road map we have and we trust it. And so we cobble together strategies to preserve and protect our communities and cultural heritage. These essays and interviews are a compendium of those strategies and the challenges Native people face at Bears Ears and across this country. I hope they inspire you to support these efforts and to take up this fight, too.

ORIGIN STORIES

/ INTERVIEWS WITH
BEARS EARS INTER-TRIBAL
COALITION ORGANIZERS

GETTING HEALED BY HEALING THE LAND

INTERVIEW WITH JONAH YELLOWMAN
BY JACQUELINE KEELER

MY NAME IS JONAH YELLOWMAN. I'M FROM MONUMENT
Valley, Utah. My clan is *Todichini nishli*. I'm a spiritual advisor for
the Utah Diné Bikéyah. I've been working with them for almost
seven years trying to designate the land that we use all the time
as a national monument so our people back home, so we can use
it every day how we always have. This is our way of life as being
a Native, what we do, gather wood and things like that. Our way
of life is like that, you know. Herbs for ceremonials and even food
for our daily use and basket weaving. We got all that up there
and then we've got hunting—those kind of things, you know. As
an organization we want to protect that land and to look after it
and so we don't want to...people mistaken it like we want...they're
telling us that we're just closing it up. It's not like that. We're making it to where us Natives can go in and use it the way we always
have. To have that collaborative management, to work with one
another and with the government. It's what we're trying to do to
make that into law.

How long have Navajos been living there?

This is a public land, a federal land. It's not the reservation. We
live like there's a boundary like on that map over there. There's a
boundary line, the San Juan River, and the reservation is on the

south side and the one we're talking about, the Bears Ears, is 1.9 million acres and it sits on the north side [of the San Juan River] in southeast Utah. We have evidence of hogans sitting out there, sweat lodges, ceremonial sites. We have petroglyphs, we have sacred grounds here and there. And we have different evidence that we as a Native [people] have gone through there. There's trails, even have a kiva out there, markings of different tribes. They recognize it: all, we went through here. Different tribes they told us, too, that they have their own ways, their own plants that they have to use for their medicine. So, we're open to everybody... as you know we're not here to destroy we're here to take care of the land, we're here to talk to nature. We are close to even air you know, the holy spirit. We talk to water, we talk to plants, and as Navajo we use sandpainting to heal ourselves with and different types of herbs. We use it different ways to put it in the water to make a tea out of it or to burn it for different ceremonies. So there's a lot of uses and so we'd like to preserve that and use it as time goes on.

How do other Navajos feel about it? What is the response you get when you talk to other Navajo people about the Bears Ears National Monument proposal?

Well, when we heard they were kind of closing things off—they were limiting where we gather our firewood. We had to go so far to get our permit and sometimes, you know, just to even get medicine they were fenced off in places. You can't get through there.

Was this with the BLM?

Yeah, BLM or forestry so with that we understand what some of our leaders told us: this is what they're going to do if we don't act on it. Through that, we decided we should do something, so we told our elders and our medicine people, medicine men, road men, whoever does these rituals and ceremonials, and they said, We use that for our everyday life. What's going to happen if we close it up? We need to keep it—that's the only thing we have. We can't just lose it and just forget about. We got to keep our language, too, alive. We got to keep our traditions alive, our cultures and our philosophies, our old stories, we got to keep it going. We got to continue on with our plants and all kinds of different things. Even our water—we got to keep it clean. We got to keep our air clean.

> **So living on the land brings those stories out to share with the next generation?**

Yes. Living back home—in some places most of my relatives out there have electricity, running water. Where I live it's different. I don't even have that yet. So that makes it different from the way I think about it because I got to have wood. Where I live we don't have wood. I have to travel at least twenty to thirty miles to the top of the ridge towards Bears Ears—that's where we gather wood. I have to travel at least about an hour and a half drive to go get a permit [from the US Forest Service] just to get wood for my own to cook with, or sometimes I use propane. Sometimes when they want ceremonies done. Like I said, I'm a spiritual advisor, leader. I have to have wood to conduct my prayer services. That's how I use that. So I got to have that. Even when you put up a sweat you got to go up there and get your wood, get your sage and different types of scent or different types of ingredient to mix with the water.

> **With this new Bears Ears Monument proposal, will you have a much more direct say—a seat at the table?**

Yeah, we're going to be sitting right across like the way we're talking now. We're going to be talking about we want this, we want that. And if they say you can't go over here we say, why? We have to have an explanation from you. If they had their limits we can say, why? Because we live that land. Our headsman Chief Manuelito was born there. So, we're tied to that land way long, we got a history to that. People don't look at it like that but Bít'aa'níí diné, he's that [Manuelito's clan].

I saw Navajos protesting at Window Rock saying they don't want the Bears Ears monument. What is that about?

I guess they don't understand. They misunderstood what we are saying. They don't see it like the way we're trying to tell them. That's where we don't understand them, too. What are you saying? We don't understand you, too. Then at the end they will say, "We support Bears Ears. We want to make it a conservation area." So what's really the difference?

Utah Diné Bikéyah is like the founder. We started this organization. And we talked with the BLM, national forestry, the ones take care of that land, and we told them what we wanted and they agreed with the way they see it—the way we see it. And then, different things occurred when we were going with our proposal. That's when the coalition started. We're the grassroots [Utah Diné Bikéyah] and they're [Bears Ears Inter-Tribal Coalition] the one doing all the government to government facilitation for us.

I heard 1,300 local Navajo people wrote letters in support of Bears Ears to D.C.

Yeah, they did.

How many Navajo people are there in the seven Navajo chapters on Bears Ears?

In our chapter around five hundred. Every chapter there it varies though. Not everyone goes to those kinds of meetings. They want to know tomorrow—what did everybody say? They want you to tell them. They don't go to the meetings.

What is it like working with other tribes like the Ute tribe and the Hopi tribe?

It's interesting. We never did this. See like when you go back to your father's [reservation]? Is it different?

Yes, the Yankton Sioux reservation is very different than the Navajo Nation.

When I go over there and have a meeting with different Hopi or the Utes, the way they see it, the way they have their stories, how they go about their ceremonies, how they look at it from their side, it's very interesting. It's like you share stories with them and it seems like to me in all the coalition the young people are very bright, got the know-how. They are very special individuals, they are being picked. That's the way I feel about them. They are very special and important people.

Me, I'm just a spiritual advisor. I take care of the ceremonial part, the prayer, those kind of things. When I see we need some protection prayer or some kind of a guidance, I go to my medicine people and I say, can you help us guiding them and helping them along? Those guys [the young people] they do all the paperwork—I'm the lazy guy. They sit down and they write them out and they [are] moving the paper.

How do you think Navajo prayers are different from Christian prayers? How do they relate to the land more directly?

Christian prayers they go direct, "Dear Heavenly Father." Navajos they go to where they're connected to: Mother Earth, Father Sky, holy mountain or holy water, morning dawn or darkness they go like that. Then everything that they use they talk to it. White corn pollen, yellow corn, our Talking God. Even the four directions [says them in Navajo and lists the sacred mountains]. Those kinds, that's how it's different like that.

So, it's very placed in the landscape, with the mountains and the rivers. It's a different way of thinking about how you are sacred in the environment— how you are in the environment, you as a person...

The way I was, the way I learned, that's the way I was taught. My father was a medicine man as a stargazer and a five-night singer and he taught me a little bit about how to do my prayers and that's how I do my prayers. Even my songs are like that.

My grandpa has a riding song he sang and I guess he sort of turned it into a sacred song. He sang it at our wedding as a blessing because he was a cowboy and so he was always on his horse and had this song he always sang. He was a hand trembler [Navajo diagnostician].

You learn from that, from a patient, every time you do a ceremony for somebody. It adds on to your belief, it adds on to a story you might be praying about using a story, a trail to walk through.

It's very much like how you move through the environment. Your prayers...I know like Christian prayers, "Give me this, I want this..." but this is more like calling upon different parts of the environment to help you, even ants.

The animal people were the ones in need of help when they called upon the humans to come and help them. That's how I look at it. And so, that's where the Asdzáá nádleehé [the goddess, Changing Woman] was brought and then bore Naayéé'neizghání do Tóbá-jíshchíní [Navajo Warrior Twins]. That's where it all started. And they helped. They got rid of all these monsters. The animal people is the one that did that. So if you look at it that way then you know you are connected somewhere through nature. Then why your prayers are like this and why you talk to those things.

One time I went to Westminster College and I said, "You know you heard this before: Indians are crazy, they will talk to anything." It's true. We're not crazy. I think we're very civilized—how we do our prayers. We come down to the nitty gritty. Even the little stone we pick it up and talk to it as an herb, as a mineral and make an offering. That's how precious we think about these things and we make that offering.

> **Do you think that really changes how you relate to the land? I was reading about white folks, I think it was in Blanding, Utah, and they were going and taking artifacts out of the site and selling them or keeping them. I know my mom, once she took us to Mesa Verde and when we got to Cameron [Arizona] her parents were really upset because they said you should never go there. We had to get a ceremony and everything because you're not supposed to touch these things. And it's such a different way of looking at the environment and everything in it. But in white culture they don't have anything like that. It's all there for the taking.**

Yeah. Just by telling these kinds of stories...all the things we talk about, like you, reporter or writer. I tell them my stories or what my elders told me. I don't just make these things up. I learn it from my people, the stories they talk about, and through my prayers when I go to these ceremonies and I listen to what they got to say. How they look at it and how I look at it and I put them together and it makes me understand more about who I am and how I've got to have respect for nature. You have to know who you are first. That's the reason why I said who I was, who I was born for, who my *cheiis* are, my *nalis*. I start from there and from there everything just falls in for you. That's what I was told. Know yourself first, who you are first, then you understand all these other things that we talk about. That's where I think we all need to learn.

We're here to take care of it. We're here to look after it. We're here to preserve it, and our medicine people, when they go and get something for a ceremony, they go over there and they'll talk to the plant or whatever they are going to use. If they are going to cut it, they always put corn pollen on it. They put it back together. Wherever they dig around they smooth it out and leave it like the way it is and they walk away from it. We just don't dig it out and make a big hole and just leave it. We don't do that. So, that's who we are as a Native American Indian people. That's who we are. We are here to take care of and look after it. If you take care of it and look after it, it's going to take care of you. You're going to get healed from it and you're going to heal the land, too, like that.

So protecting the land—it seems like it's a huge area, 1.9 million acres. I've been talking to First Nations in Canada and there's this group called the Coastal Guardian Watchmen and they are First Nations, there are several of them in British Columbia, and they actually have their own patrol boats and they go out and they patrol their traditional territories looking for hunters, people entering their territory to hunt bears or to disrupt the environment. They also go into the archaeological sites. They protect those sites and I just don't think that we have that here in the United States. We don't have a group like that that patrols these sites.

That's the sad part. This is going to help us. If we go through with this then we can say, hey, this is a special area, this is a spiritual [place]. Go over here or just have respect. That's what we're after.

It's just really hard because the land is so vast. And I don't know how many federal agents are out there, maybe three or two? It's hard for them to be everywhere and see everything.

A lot of things are interesting so far, what we learn. Ourselves—we are educating ourselves by doing this. I never knew that much when I started talking to these people who know more. Medicine men and roadmen and whoever knows about herbs. So far I know a little bit—that's what I tell my roadmen, my medicine people, they know a whole lot more. They've got stories, "This is what happened at that time." They're going to sing a song and they'll stop for a little while and they'll tell you, through that creation, this song was sung at that particular time and this was why that is a word. They'll tell you like that and they'll continue on singing again a song where they will stop again and they'll tell you the same thing again—this is why this happened, this is why the words are like this. Those kind, you know. I learned from my elders like that.

I hope this, what we're doing, will come about, come to pass. It's going to heal a lot of people. It's going to enlighten their life, their outlook in life. They're going to know there's still hope up ahead.

What do you think of the pushback you are getting? You've got Senator Hatch? You've got him all riled up. They're throwing hundreds of thousands of dollars...

They always say that my people, you know us—you're as my *nali* [he's referring to my clan; I am his paternal grandmother clan-wise] —they'll tell us, if there's going to be a good turn-out, if it's for the best, it's always going to be something like that. It's going to challenge you. That's the way it goes. But you learn from that, from that, too. After you put all of your stories together.

FIGHTING FOR THE LAND AND BUILDING HEALING FROM WITHIN

INTERVIEW WITH REGINA LOPEZ-WHITESKUNK
BY JACQUELINE KEELER

ABOUT SIX YEARS AGO, A GRASSROOTS GROUP OF NAVAJOS called Utah Diné Bikéyah came together and organized. They actually started this whole movement for permanent protection of the Bears Ears region. Originally, they tried to work within the public process in San Juan County. When it appeared that their interests were being downplayed by the county, they stepped it up by going to several tribes and recruiting the tribal groups to the table to have a conversation for greater protection of the area. And in July 2015, several tribes met. We felt at that point, this was a conversation that we needed to have collectively as sovereign voices—a sovereign voice to elevate the conversation to a government-to-government discussion.

On July 15th, five tribes, the Ute Mountain Ute, Navajo, Hopi, Pueblo, Zuni, and the Ute Indian tribe of Utah, all formally agreed to become what would be known as the Bears Ears Inter-Tribal Coalition. Other tribes were also invited, but they chose to remain as support and have helped us by providing support resolutions and letters to the movement.

I was a part of that initial inter-tribal meeting so I've been involved from the inception of the coalition. Prior to this project, aside from seeing the landscape, I didn't really understand what Bears Ears really meant to us (the Ute Mountain Ute tribe). Since the conversation we had that day, I really delved into it and have had numerous conversations with elders and former leaders my father used to work with including the late Chairman House (Ernest House Sr.). I spent a lot of time talking to him about this, as well as with my own family. What I found out was that during the period the federal government was putting different tribes on reservations, the Ute Mountain Ute tribe was looking at housing its headquarters in the Allen Canyon area. If it hadn't been for the settlers and the Mormons expressing a desire to farm that area, and having settled and homesteaded in those areas, my tribe's headquarters could have quite possibly been right in the proposed area of the Bears Ears National Monument.

That was very interesting to find out that bit of information but even before the reservation years, my people have looked upon the Bears Ears area as a sacred site. And personally, in my own family, my grandfather was a medicine man, and he would go to Bears Ears and camp to collect herbs or provide services to those that needed it—whether they were Ute or Navajos. Whoever needed his help, he was there for them, and if people needed him to go to them, he had almost like a little mobile medical office, I guess you could say, and so he would provide those services. For those who could come to him, he helped but if they couldn't travel then he would go down into the Monument Valley area and help those that needed it.

And so, for my family, Bears Ears was a very central location for us. I've had other grandparents and family members who were raised in that area. Families that can show where their watermelon patch used to be or their orchards, where they grew up as children running and playing in the meadows and down near where the water was. They can tell of when they had to haul water from those waterways back to their camps where they were living. And my grandmother Stella Eyetoo can tell stories about their lives in

Bears Ears right to the point where the federal government came and took them away to boarding school. So they were taken away from that area as young children. My grandmother Stella is still alive, she's ninety-four years old for the fifth year in a row now!

I like to keep the discussion about protecting Bears Ears positive. I believe visiting negative aspects like historical atrocities won't accomplish anything, but at the same time, this painful history is always at the back of our minds even if it's not at the tip of our tongue. Still, at this year's Utah Governor Herbert's Native American Summit, I found his bold statement of "We, the settlers" ironic because when you really think about it in the context of time, the settlers and the people that exist in these geographical locations are only inhabitants, very recent inhabitants. When you look back and really delve into the history since their arrival—yes, the Utes were driven out of those areas by settlers. The Puebloan people had already migrated away from the Bears Ears area at a much earlier time so they didn't have that negative interaction with the settlers. Although, they may have been driven out by climate changes, or other changes beyond their control. So, we've all experienced having to leave the Bears Ears but that does not change, unfortunately, the fact that non-Indians are very, very recent inhabitants.

The boundaries for the national monument that have been established in the proposal by the coalition are very much representative of the cultural resources in those areas. This is how those boundaries were established. I've said it many times—we just didn't take a coloring crayon and decide: "This looks like a nice shade, let's go draw these lines." No, they're based upon cultural resources along those boundaries. We'd love for it to be greater but the complications of private landowners and various other reasons help to dictate where some of those boundary lines exist within our proposal.

The county commissioners and even just local people, they have a very strong view as to why they feel justified in feeling the way they do. Apparently, to them, their contemporary existence has more value than that of Indigenous people who have long been in the area. I still find it strange they feel so compelled to say they are entitled to this land because their settler families came in and homesteaded the area. We certainly don't see it that way. We want to be able to come together and they hold their opinions at such a high level that it is almost unworkable. Our attempts at conversations with the county and the state have been incredibly contentious because of this. In contrast, when we have conversations with the federal agencies and, specifically, the White House administration, they are far more open to listening and seeing some of the solutions we have.

So it was this big difference in attitude and reception which led us to decide to abandon the process of working on the Public Lands Initiative proposed by Rep. [Rob] Bishop and supported by the state and county. On December 31st [2015] ...a delegation from the legislature [was supposed to] meet with us for a meeting—and then in the eleventh hour they canceled on us for whatever reason—we just felt we'd dealt with a lot of their cancellations and rescheduling and now we're at a point where we've got to make a decision. Do we ride this legislative process out, which could lead us down the road of three years or more? Or do we make a decision and turn to an executive process and begin lobbying the president to utilize the Antiquities Act? We talked about it a good portion of the day and we said, you know, it's now or never. Our people have waited a long time and they put us in these positions to make tough decisions like this. We had to ask ourselves: Are we up to this? And we decided by a consensus of the group there that day that we were. We're going to go the executive route and we're going to put our teeth in that campaign.

The proposal we developed is absolutely unique because the five tribes that came together to organize this group really, truly represent a sense of healing from within. When Navajos and Hopis can sit together in one room and have the same common goals—likewise, the Navajo and the Ute. These tribes on both sides have been traditionally, great enemies for many generations. This is actually a phenomenal change—that we can come to see something in common instead of seeing our differences. Instead of focusing on the generations of disagreement and to come to the understanding that this is a new time, a new day. How things were dealt with in the development of this monument proposal and how they are resolved are completely different from the way they used to be. I recall the day that we came together and said we're going to do this. I remember one of the discussions, specifically, was we would leave all other politics outside of the ring when we gather to speak about Bears Ears. And don't get me wrong, we still have our individual politics within neighboring tribes. I mean, Hopi and Navajo still have their dealings. The Utes and the Navajos, we still have our dealings, and a lot of times they're not very easy to deal with but we've worked really hard to keep those politics, that sort of politics, outside the door when we come together. That was just a mutual agreement and we've held pretty respectably true to our word from that day forward.

And the consensus process between each tribe has been good in that we have talked things through until we understood or we agreed—but at the same time it does take time and it does take patience. The whole idea of seeking to fully understand each other in order for us to agree upon something is good, but it is a very long, painstaking process sometimes. Which led to a lot of our meetings throughout the year being very long meetings. We've gone between eight to ten hours talking about one issue and really making sure that we all have an understanding of whatever point we made. And the discussion regarding the collaborative management piece—that was a very long day, and at the end of the day we walked away knowing that we had put together a strong, collaborative management piece for our proposal and had really put in every effort to maintain a perspective that would be legal and be sought after under the Antiquities Act.

It's been an amazing process. I have taken my youngest son out to one of our gatherings out at Bears Ears. He's also accompanied me on a couple of our meetings at various locations—we take turns hosting the meeting between the five tribes, so we travel out to each of the reservations. My son has sat through the process. He's visited the proposed national monument's physical location and he's amazed at the fact that five tribes could come together to protect something so beautiful. You know if you visit Bears Ears you cannot get a cell signal. If you do it's pretty sketchy, and that represents to me the simplicity Native Americans have been raised around and that being still, being still out in what is now called the wilderness but that was our way, our home, our way of life. That's how we existed and to be able to find places like that? My son was, at the time that we visited Bears Ears, sixteen, and now he's nineteen and he's still enthralled about the places that we visited and the leaders that continue to speak so strongly to preserve these sacred places. And so, for my family and my son, it has been a truly valuable experience to witness and to be a part of this. We've asked him for his perspective during our meetings and we were able to hear the youth voice and this helped us to maintain a certain perspective and it's a blessing.

The most valuable part I found in working with the other tribal leaders is just getting to know one another, and being able to value our individual differences, and embracing and celebrating those differences. A couple of weeks ago, Senator [Mike] Lee hosted his version of a public hearing in Blanding, but we had to decline—I had a commitment to attend a sun dance ceremony. My co-chair, Alfred from Hopi, as well as Carlton from the Pueblo of Zuni, we all had ceremonial commitments, and we literally could not attend those meetings because we had to honor our commitments traditionally. That's been the most spectacular part of this whole process of participating is really understanding each other and our differences and valuing them. I didn't know about the processes the men had to go through in the kivas and it's been enjoyable learning new things about one another but even more so, we've become like a family. I remember the first day and meeting everyone and how I was really not really comfortable—especially being the only female, it was really uncomfortable (laughs). I would be in a room of guys, but I became like a little sister to them and now, when we're not involved in our discussion, I get teased like a little sister. It's humor—humor is always a big aspect of our culture and we have great times during the meetings and great discussions. Even after the meetings when we have dinner and before we all go to our home, we have such camaraderie for one another. It's been amazing.

I've learned a lot—I think we've all learned a lot about the federal systems and policies all the way up to the White House. We've learned how each of the state governments differs. We also learned how each of our tribal government differs and operates. So, it's been such a learning experience that has become very valuable to each of us. When we return and go back to our own council, our own communities, we take a little bit of that with us and it lends to such a richer experience as a tribal leader.

One of the other events that I was able to attend recently was the meeting of outdoor recreational groups in Salt Lake City. San Juan County represents a huge area for outdoor recreationalists, as well as the amount of money it brings into the state economy. A national monument under our proposal will definitely increase and enhance the management of those opportunities. We also want opportunities, permanent opportunities, for monument staff and other businesses that may develop and provide permanent positions to locals in the area. Positions that would be beyond what energy development provides. A lot of those energy resource jobs are only temporary construction positions but when you start to look at permanent jobs and then you start to look at the long-term impact to the economy, that's where there's a big difference.

And San Juan County residents that are opposed to a national monument, I'm not quite sure they've taken the time to really delve into the proposal. If they did, they will see that we're not trying to take something away from them, but we want to see it preserved in a responsible manner. We're not only thinking of today, we're thinking of generations down the road. We're thinking of what will be here for our great-grandchildren. How will they know what the history of the land is if we don't make sure that it is preserved in the right way? That they will have the same opportunities that we do and those people who recreate out there.

I'm going to speak specifically to the Bears Ears area—especially the buttes. As traditional people, we always have a focal point and it starts at the center, and I think things radiate out from the center of that energy. We have to make sure that heals and it has the opportunity to heal and to be available down the road. It radiates out when you start to look at the land, the geographical make-up of the area, the different terrain. We have waterways, we have meadows, we have different ecological systems out there. If we can preserve it, we can help maintain the health of many different ecological systems that are very dependent on what exists there now. The minute we alter it in any way, we affect something down the road. The fish, the health of the fish in the riverbeds, every aspect of the land serves a purpose. It all plays into making sure that we're able to teach and continue to teach our culture, which is tied to the land, down, down the road. If the land gets destroyed, we won't have a tool or a mechanism to teach the next generation. We all learn, we're all products of the land, we learn from it. We know how our ancestors adjusted to the adversities they faced, but if the land is plundered, we lose that knowledge because the land is our teacher.

Even today, every, every time I hear something new and great—like the re-discovery of a bean species or something our ancestors learned to grow during a great drought historically—we wouldn't make those discoveries if it gets all destroyed and thrown in a pile of rubbish that the oil and gas industry piles over to the side and calls "reclamation." It takes a page out of our history.

Tribal nations need greater input, we need to—and this is one of the things that has really come out of the discussion of the Bears Ears and our proposal that we've put out there, is that we don't want just consultation. We want greater input. We want a greater say on the decisions being made. During the Gold King Mine spill, we were basically a little checkmark on a box and if one of the tribes did not bring more attention to what happened, the federal authorities would have overlooked the fact that the Ute Mountain Ute tribe was also [affected] by this. Maybe not to the degree or in the immediate way the Navajo Nation or Southern Ute were, but we were actually one of the three tribes that are in direct contact with the toxic spill at both ends of it. Because my tribe has a water interest in this, just directly off the Animus River in the Durango area, and we have water rights in the San Juan River which swings up through the Colorado side near the Four Corners Monument. I was very vocal about that to the EPA and Gina McCarthy [EPA administrator] when she visited the area. I said, you guys had better go back and do some homework and research because you really have a greater group of people out there who are not just "stakeholders," but sovereign nations. You need to make sure that we have greater input than just some sort of consultation and a checkmark on a box.

I believe that the joint federal/tribal commission that we propose within the Bears Ears National Monument proposal will provide more input in regard to scrutinizing projects and expansion of development. I know, for example, right now, we have one mine that is looking to expand three times the size of what it is now. One of the areas of Rep. Bishop's Public Lands Initiative proposal that has not been made clear to the public is that Bishop didn't feel the need to contact the Ute Mountain Ute tribe, specifically. We propose every tribe, especially those tribes that are represented on the commission, would definitely have a voice and input. In this way, we'd be able to ensure the process of evaluating cultural resources and ensure environmental impact statements are actually done. Some of these things are done so lightly right now that they are merely just a checkbox on a grocery list, and if it gets done correctly or not, we're not sure who checks or validates that. And then they just move on to the next process on down the line. The commission would scrutinize some of the procedures. Also, the commission would be able to bring forth traditional knowledge which doesn't always get considered in a lot of decision-making conversations. I think that's one of the key areas that our commission would be able to provide—a strong bridge between Western science and evidence and traditional knowledge.

My great-grandfather was a medicine man and he passed away a little before I was actually born but my grandmother grew up in the Bears Ears area, and she is getting quite old—I never really got to be out there while they collected the herbs and whatnot. But what I do know is when I have gone out with my grandparents and my parents to do traditional collection of different things it's always interesting because it is accompanied by a story. It always gets accompanied with a process—a protocol of showing gratitude and speaking to the plant, to the spirit of the plant, and it always gets accompanied by prayer and some sort of offering of thanks. We always want to encourage those little spirits to grow because we know that, especially within things as delicate as herbs, they're not always going to be in the same place every time. Sometimes they travel to different places and you have to really be aware and know what you're looking for. And they're not always going to come in super abundant supplies. You just take what you need and leave the rest. Those are some of the teachings that my grandparents and my parents have taught me.

Visiting and getting to know some of the other tribes and how they've approached the area and what it means to them has been really exciting because their teachings and their values and how they perform them, parallels exactly what one tribe or another may also practice. That's been something that has been interesting to learn along the way, is what things we all do the same as well.

I was actually really excited for the opportunity to be able to provide testimony in Salt Lake to one of the [legislative] committees because I had just a week prior to that testified in Denver before a committee there, and because I thought not very many people get to testify in two states within two weeks' time. I was very, very shocked by the way I was treated by the Utah legislature. I felt belittled and disrespected because the committee cut me off, didn't let me finish my statement, and then asked some really off-the-wall questions that were not even related to the issue. I approached that situation with the way I was taught, to provide the grace that I needed to. I didn't respond back in a negative manner. But it left me feeling very disrespected as a tribal leader because we grow up with strong values that when somebody is speaking you do not interrupt, you let them finish what they're saying. You do that even more so for elders and leaders, and I didn't feel that sentiment was provided to me. And I left that event feeling not too great. It was entirely a night and day experience between testifying in Colorado and testifying in Utah.

I imagine the Navajo Nation president probably had a similar feeling to what I did [when he spoke at Bears Ears and was shouted down by Navajo supporters of Rep. Bishop's Public Land Initiative that includes a huge giveaway of Ute land totaling hundreds of thousands of acres]. I think given the circumstances he did very well. He continued and finished his statement, but I think in true respect for one another, some of the people have really lost their traditional values and direction in the defense of their position and opinions. I was shocked that they could have done that to their tribal president.

BRINGING THE YOUTH BACK TO THE REALITY OF THE NATURAL WORLD

INTERVIEW WITH WILLIE GRAYEYES
BY JACQUELINE KEELER

What is most important about protecting Bears Ears?

I THINK THE HEALING ASPECTS OF PRESERVING THE LAND is what should be taken much more seriously. It doesn't matter where on the bracket that you are, if you will. If you're on this side, or this side, or down here, or down there, there needs to be a healing process. Today throughout the world, countries, states, there are parties fighting against each other. Why? Wars going on in countries...is it necessary to dominate other people? Or to find some sort of peace? That is my question. Today wars, fighting are going on—why? Because land or religion—those two are the only things that create war and we [Utah Diné Bikéyah] are in a state of...verbal war between our organization and the state, the county. And it's because of the land. From their perspective they want to control it. Control it by virtue of the fact that they are a dominant society and a dominant government.

There are other people within the world who pursue peace and love. These are the people, I think, that we are in accord with. We're looking at the situation we are in—and of course, you could respond with the same kind of hateful actions [of our opponents] but we resort to doing things in the way that we feel it should be handled—in a peaceful, healing way.

I think support for our proposal is going well. We have the support of the public, but if we do get President Obama to agree to create the national monument, I know there's going to be a lot of negative pushback from the state government all the way down to the county. But I don't know how long a person or a government can keep up those types of negative attitudes or behaviors. It boils down to some underlying issues. Right now, we are seeing only superficial displays of these attitudes and behavior.

When getting down to the roots of the issue, you might want to do an assessment of the social system underlying these governments [the state and the county] to find out what their positions are on these issues. Why? It would be an interesting assessment because the underlying issue—what I anticipate or assume—is that the energy companies are paying these politicians to pursue developments in culturally-sensitive areas we don't want disturbed. That's all there is to it and there's no healing in that type of economic development if you come in to disturb an area.

When I was in Washington, we were interviewed by the national newscasts and I said, "If you guarantee me you can take a grain of sand, remove it and pile it over here and when you finish with the project you can pick up that grain and put it exactly the way it was...that will give you the leeway to do whatever you please." But only one person can do that. Some humans possibly can do it if they have the full belief in that and practice and share love and healing for others. But I believe no human beings can do that because they are all on one side of the track.

What do you think dominant society can learn from Navajo ways of being on the land? How do you think it's different?

I think a lot about human relationships to the land. Right now, there is what they call economic-driven concepts. Everybody wants to say, "I have a goal to make a million dollars." That's all there is, people trying to get to heaven on a pile of money. They don't see themselves and are keeping up with the Begays or Yazzies [common Navajo surnames]. In dominant society, it's the Joneses and somebody else living down the road...when they get behind or somebody is getting little bit ahead of them—it's very uncomfortable for them. And Navajos, they're picking up those types of practices and concepts. They would rather see a brand-new Silverado four-wheel drive, even if their house is just a shack. I drive a 1995 truck. I can get here and there just as comfortably. I don't look at time.

Those are some of the developments and learned behavior that is destroying the stability of our families, community, and our [Navajo] nation. Then again, what also comes into play is making a fast buck—money. The fastest money-making business is the drug business and it is underground. Those are the things that are going on at the same time the societal change is occurring. These are the things we are learning from dominant society—everything. We have gangs on the reservation, we have drug dealers. You don't see it but they are there. The younger people, younger generations, are threatening their grandmothers who receive Social Security benefits, taking their money and spending it.

These are the types of behaviors that are being seen on the Navajo Nation, and what we are seeking to do with the Bears Ears National Monument is to stabilize our community and to bring the youth back to the reality of the natural world. We want to teach them how to utilize these resources in a way that not only benefits them in their pocket, but spiritually. To teach them that this water from this spring is pure—it's good to drink. This earth over here will heal you. It is a healing substance that will not give you headaches but will clean you from the inside out and give you better health. All that in association with spirituality, psychological understanding, enhancement, and physiological good health. And it's not only health but it's the interrelationship, the psychological part that creates a good relationship. This circle of relationships continues a cycle where the youth know how to protect these natural resources and how to utilize it in a sustainable way. Environmentally, you got clean air, clean water, beautiful landscape—a place to kneel down and pray to the god of your choice.

Companies are out there selling their expertise. The engineering world is a costly thing but people need to understand these corporations that come out here to mine the natural resources, they will buy you certain things but they will themselves profit to an even greater degree. When they first came here, there was no reclamation—reclaiming of the surface, the natural resources. They took, they dug, they made the money, and they leave—that's what's happened.

Now, we're educated as Navajos—we know what's going to be destroyed. We know what's going on and we're looking at more positive approaches to economic development. I think that's the difference between the more harmonious approach and the "hit-and-run and never come back and say it has to be reclaimed" approach. At Tuba City [Navajo Nation city in Arizona] I always say there's the *Yei 'tsoh*, the big monster, that is lying right there. There is one over here in Tuba City, one in Mexican Hat—that's where they buried the *yeii*. The *yeii* is the giant, a destructive monster the Twins [Monster Slayer (Nayéé' Neizghání) and Born For Water (Tó Bá Jíshchíní)] had to kill to make our world, this world safe. So, that type of thinking is like that and very important.

**How do you think your activism in this has changed
your notion of what it means to be Navajo?**

I think, overall, this experience educated me in terms of understanding how the dominant system works—the state, federal, and the counties. I understand it now but I don't know if I will be involved with educating the public rather than working with kids. The idea is to spread what we have learned and to educate a number of members of the community and have them carry on this work.

**You've been going to chapter houses to present the Bears Ears proposal.
Which chapter houses did you go to?**

Well, not necessarily chapter houses. Some of our presentations, for instance, were at Chinle [another Navajo city in the central Navajo Nation]. It was for "Older American Day." They were celebrating and we were invited in Chinle, Arizona. We had, I estimate, about four hundred people and they filled a gym and they knew about our projects and they encouraged us. "Yes, you're doing a good job. Keep up the good work and we support you!" Those are some of their expressions of support. I tried to explain things so they would understand in detail the project's focus: why, where, who, and so forth. All about how we wanted to establish permanent protection of the land. I think that's the key thing people need to hear—when you just go in there and just talk about the why, when, and who you leave out something.

**What was the response? What were questions other Navajos
had to ask about Bears Ears?**

I could pat myself on the back if there was hardly any questions because I did a good job. But I figure there is going to be opposition questions like yesterday [at a panel about Bears Ears he was on in Salt Lake City]. The gentleman in the back did not catch me off guard when he said, "Why are you involved [with the Bears Ears National Monument proposal] when the Navajo Nation was paid for that land back in the 1980's?" "1984, in fact," I told him. I was on the Navajo Nation Council—I was on the budget and finance committee at that time when the federal government says okay, we will settle this land claim issue for $32 million.

The thing that he was trying to do was to possibly corner me. And I said, that's not the issue. The issue is that this is BLM land and BLM land is public land. Anybody throughout the United States has a say about public land. If they have a better land-use plan they can propose it. And this is what it is, our proposal is a land-use plan. So I offered him a pamphlet of what is allowable according to the national monument proposal. My grandpa over here [indicates Jonah Yellowman, a clan relative] went after the brochures and he offered one to him but he wouldn't accept it. So, when I got one I went up to him and said, here it is, and he took it.

> **So, there's a small contingent of Navajos who don't want to know any more than they already know?**

The attempt was to derail the whole thing but the thing is...the federal payment of the Navajo land claim for the Bears Ears area is not relevant to our proposal for a co-managed national monument on public lands.

> **In coalitions like this, you sometimes see local stakeholders, like white landowners, ranchers, joining with tribes. Have you seen this on the Bears Ears issue?**

I have no idea but there is support, I think. As far as I know, we

[Utah Diné Bikéyah] are the only local grassroots organization that has pursued a project of this magnitude. If we were elected officials, we couldn't have formed the Inter-Tribal Coalition. We would still be talking government to government with the Department of the Interior.

Navajos make up the majority in that county, I understand.

The county is...the makeup is fifty-two to fifty-four percent Navajo. That's also a lawsuit that was filed, a class-action lawsuit that they are monopolizing county elections, including the county commissioner election and how they were splitting the vote. Navajo voters could form a block to vote but they are split so they cannot have a majority in more than one of the three districts.

Do you think that would change? Navajos having more representation in county government?

I think there needs to be allowance, sooner or later. For instance, like Navajo County and Coconino County and Apache Counties, they have Navajos that are sitting on the Board of Supervisors so even at the state level—we are getting in there. So not too long from here I see someone running for the state representative or the Senate up here. I mean there are educated Navajos.

GREENTHREAD: BEARS EARS TO BROOKLYN

ALASTAIR BITSOI

IT'S EASY TO GET CONSUMED BY THE CHAOS OF NEW York City. To keep connected with the natural world, my mind often lingers on moments spent at the Bears Ears buttes.

Bears Ears reminds me of my purpose in life and affirms my identity as a Navajo being—a 31-year-old man whose *Tó'áhání* (Near-To-Water) clan is represented by the Cougar as protector, and whose *Kinyaa'áanii* (Towering House People) bloodline is protected by the Bear. This spiritual connection of the Cougar and Bear is remembered in traditional stories about my Navajo clans is critical to my identity and to my survival in this global society.

When my mind needs nature-feeding, I find a city park with fertile ground to pinch dirt or inhale some elements of what I think is fresh air. If access is made impossible because of the daily grind of graduate school work at New York University, then my mind finds that connection in my recollection of the various Navajo and Native American Church ceremonies I've attended throughout my life.

Other times, I think about other intertribal ceremonies, such as the Bear Dance of the Ute people, or the slew of deer that grazed near family camps scattered below the Bears Ears buttes—what we call *Shásh Jaa'*—that mid-July when the Bears Ears Inter-Tribal Coalition launched itself as an official stakeholder to a proposal that will protect 1.9 million acres of ancestral lands.

The cultural significance of each spirit expressed in our daily lives—human and animal—is honored at ceremonies like the Navajo Fire Dance, which cites wildlife as having healing properties. Amongst Navajos, the Bear is cited ritually as a healer and protector for the afflicted. Because of that cultural role, the protection and conservation of the Bears Ears buttes in southeastern Utah seems natural. All proposals led by Native American tribes need to be considered within their cultural context.

And, specifically at Bears Ears, this spiritual connection between humans and animals includes other living organisms and cultural sites presently under siege by water contamination from proposed natural resource exploitation, looting of cultural artifacts, and overgrazing, among other environmental health issues. The voices of tribal leaders such as Evangeline Grey of Westwater, Utah, an isolated community of the Aneth Chapter in the Navajo Nation, must be heard. "If Bears Ears continues to be another open area for miners and for oil and gas…the whole place is going to be ruined," Grey said. "This is why we are asking the president to sign this into a monument. That way it can be protected."

I first learned about the 1.9-million-acre Bears Ears land proposal as a reporter for the *Navajo Times*. But it was not until I visited this pristine landscape two summers ago as a freelance writer for the *Advocate* magazine (a publication of the Grand Canyon Trust) that I understood the importance of protecting this cultural territory.

My piece, published in the *Advocate*, essentially told the tribal perspective of the Bears Ears proposal, and why it is necessary for tribes to unite to co-manage 1.9 million acres as a US presidential national monument designation under the Antiquities Act of 1906.

Being exposed to the lay of the land—including an aerial flight of the red canyons—the majestic San Juan River and every living creature in between, inspired me to continue telling the Navajo connection to Bears Ears. In *Red Rock Testimony: Three Generations of Writers Speak on Behalf of Utah's Public Lands*, published by Torrey House Press, I recollect my personal experience of visiting Bears Ears in a piece entitled "Shásh Jaa' Follows Wherever I Go." The short piece tells of how my Navajo connection to this land is alive, even in New York City.

While sipping a cup of Navajo tea, which grows prolifically across the Navajo Nation and in the Bears Ears region, on a cold November night in my Brooklyn apartment, I am reminded that this herbal tea and other medicinal plants play a critical role in Navajo healing practices, such as the Navajo Blessing Way.

Known as greenthread (*Thelesperma*), the wild tea grows among the mountainous knolls, evergreens, and wildlife of the Bears Ears region. My memories of this place keep me connected on the Navajo path of *Hózhó* (beauty), while studying public health at NYU in Manhattan, thousands of miles away.

At NYU, the Bears Ears connection is also alive. It runs deep in two doctoral students I know here at NYU, Angelo Baca and Teresa Montoya, both Navajo. Baca is from Aneth, Utah, and Montoya is from Window Rock, Arizona. Both, through film, are examining the impact environmental injustice has on their communities back home. A monument designation could alleviate public health issues associated with oil development on the Navajo Nation, in the communities where they were raised. Through the work of these Navajo filmmakers, I feel protected in the sense that no matter where I go, Bears Ears seems to be a topic of relevancy. This may be due to coincidence, serendipity, or even the spiritual associations of the Cougar and Bear to my clans: *Tó'áháni* and *Kinyaa'áanii*. It could be anything, but what I know is that the spirit of Bears Ears is here.

In addition, Navajo historical stories of a Navajo presence at Bears Ears inspires me to stand up and speak out for protection of this sacred land. According to Navajo historian Jennifer Nez Denetdale, Navajo Headman Chief Manuelito was born atop the Bears Ears buttes—yet more evidence of a Diné footprint prior to American colonization in this northern region of the *Diné Bikéyah* (Navajo land).

The remains of the ancient Anasazi civilization also prove the tribal connection that certain Navajo clans, the Hopi, Zuni, Utes and other tribes of the Southwest, have to the Bears Ears region. Along with ruins and pottery—now endangered by nonstop non-Native looting for cash profit—other structures, such as those once inhabited by Chief Manuelito and his Bit'ahnii Clan, are also threatened.

Thus, protective action is necessary now more than ever. After all, plants like the greenthread—wild tea—grow there. If these plants and herbs are not protected by a monument designation as proposed by the Bears Ears Inter-Tribal Coalition, then it is likely that traditional cultural knowledge could disappear as anthropogenic hazards wipe out these living spaces—and with them, knowledge systems of the natural world. These thoughts, while probably misunderstood by those who do not have a connection to the natural world, come to mind as I sip the hot tea from *Diné Bikéyah*.

It is a critical time for the Obama administration and Trump administration to exercise the use of the Antiquities Act. Designating the 1.9 million acres of ancestral tribal land as the Bears Ears National Monument allows tribes, including the Navajo, to engage for the first time with federal, state, and county as stakeholders. Tribes, who were instructed by the Creator to protect Mother Earth through their cultural practices, know how lands should be rightfully managed.

FOR THIS LAND, FOR THE DINÉ BIKÉYAH

/ACTIVISTS AND ACADEMICS SPEAK FOR BEARS EARS

DAUGHTER OF TWO LANDSCAPES

ELIZABETH WOODY

CHINLE SUMMER

Loneliness for me is being the daughter of two landscapes,
distant from the horizon circling me.
The red earth completely round.
The sky a deep bowl of turquoise overhead.
Mother and father. Loneliness
rising up like thunderheads. The rain pours over
the smooth rocks into the canyon that is familiar.

This is the road that leads to my father's home.
After twenty years I stand on the threshold of his mother's hogan.
Grandmother sits in the cool dark, out of the light
from the door and smoke hole. She talks softly
in the Diné language.

Talking to me as I grew in her warmth, my mother
lowered herself in this canyon, barefoot and unafraid.
She walked miles in high heels to church by this road
that runs alongside Canyon de Chelly.
She was a river woman walking in dust.

The Recumbent Woman whispers inside different languages.
I am one story. Beauty walked South and then North again.
Beauty sparked physical creation.

A strong and wild will draws up the land into the body.
My journey circles back, unraveling, unmaking itself
like the magnificent loom work of my grandmother's center.
My grandfather once told me, "Lizzy, I was busy singing
over there...you were here. So I came home to see you."

IN MEMORY OF
CROSSING THE COLUMBIA

For Charlotte Edwards Pitt and Charlotte Agnes Pitt

My board and blanket were Navajo,
but my bed is inside the river.
In the beads of remembrance,
I am her body in my Father's hands.
She gave me her eyes
and the warmth of basalt.
The vertebrae of her back,
my breastplate, the sturdy
belly of mountainside.

"Pahtu," he whispered in her language.
She is the mountain of change.
She is the mountain of women
who have lain as volcanoes
before men.

Red, as the women much loved,
she twisted like silvery Chinook
beyond his reach.

Dancing the Woman-Salmon dance,
there is not much time to waste.

LAND: "NÍHI KÉYAH"

LLOYD LEE

THE LAND MEANS THE WORLD TO ALL NATIVE PEOPLES of the United States. Their philosophies, origins, histories, and cultures are tied to the land. Land is more than a commodity and property for the people; it is their way of life and identity. The land is a physical, emotional, psychological, and spiritual presence for the people. The land is the core of what it means to be human and Native. Its vitality, energy, and power is reflected in the Native people's narratives.

In "Man Made of Words," N. Scott Momaday illustrates how narrative and place are interconnected for Native people:

> *I am interested in the way a man looks at a landscape and takes possession of it in his blood and brain. For this happens, I am certain, in the ordinary motion of life. None of us lives apart from the land entirely; such an isolation is unimaginable. We do not act upon a stagnant landscape, but instead are part of it. Place is created in the process of remembering and telling stories and the ability of the receiver to understand the meanings of place encapsulated in language. Key to both the spiritual and political "aspirations" of Indigenous people are the stories and imaginative acts that are dynamic interfaces, rather than methods of claiming land as a stagnant location.*

Many Native peoples, communities, and nations have been removed from their original land bases and live elsewhere. This does not mean the people have lost connection or touch with their original homelands. What it shows is the deep physical, emotional, psychological, and spiritual yearning and relation with their homeland. For Hopi, Navajo, Ute, and Zuni peoples, the Bears Ears land and the surrounding area have narratives and connections that are unbreakable and strong.

These narratives and bonds embody the identity for the Hopi, Navajo, Ute, and Zuni peoples. The Bears Ears is still a place for healing, ceremonies, the gathering of firewood, plants, and medicinal herbs, and the continuation of distinct ways of life. The land records the people's migration routes, roads, villages, communities, burial grounds, sweat lodges, petroglyphs, pictographs, home dwellings, and granaries. The people maintain and sustain their identity through land.

Bears Ears is a place for healing and educating. Native peoples have ceremonies in the area and it is a place to teach Native children the distinct ways of life representing Hopi, Navajo, Ute, and Zuni heritages. Native children learn about the meaningfulness of and connection to the land through the narratives, histories, ceremonies, traditions. All of this encompasses what is called Indigenous traditional knowledge. Indigenous traditional knowledge of the land is a core part of all Native people's identity and way of life.

Article 25 of the United Nations Declaration on the Rights of Indigenous Peoples, which the United States approved in 2010, states the following:

Indigenous peoples have the right to maintain and

strengthen their distinctive spiritual relationship with their traditionally owned or otherwise occupied and used lands, territories, waters and coastal seas and other resources and to uphold their responsibilities to future generations in this regard.

This article is designed to protect and sustain for future generations of Native peoples and all peoples a distinct knowledge and connection to land. Several other articles in the Declaration such as 26, 31, and 32 also protect Native peoples' land relations and connection.

Thousands of Hopi, Navajo, Ute, and Zuni peoples view the land as home and this perspective creates an undeniable spirit of the people and the recognition of a child to the earth and universe. The land means support, love, and a deep spiritual belonging. For instance, in Navajo, the land is referred to as "Níhi Kéyah." The English translation means "our land," and it demonstrates a monumental expression of place and being for the Navajo peoples.

The land is integral to Native identity and cultural distinctiveness. Native peoples have worked hard to sustain their original and adopted land base. The land is beyond property or simply a "reservation." It frames the world of Native peoples. The land, Níhi Kéyah, is the embodiment of the Diné people's notion of humanity and what it means to live as a human being. The land has energy, power, and provides the necessary support and love for other human beings in other places and spaces around the world.

By placing Bear Ears in federal protection, all peoples will be able to sustain and maintain a space rich in history and culture. Bears Ears National Monument can be a place where natural relations are paramount and recognized by all human beings. It can be a place where Indigenous traditional knowledge can help with land management. It can be a place where all peoples' dreams and positive energy can be appreciated, understood, and acknowledged. It can be a place and space where all can relate to one another and to the earth itself.

INDIGENOUS CULTURES, INDIGENOUS PLACES

JACQUELINE KEELER

WHAT IS THE VALUE OF CULTURE COMPARED TO THE resources that can be extracted from the land? This is at heart of the question raised when Indigenous peoples lay claim to the land because of their cultural connection to it—often in defiance of corporate and settler colonial desires to fully develop the energy or mineral or agricultural properties of that land. What is the best use of the land by human beings? Is it the cultural heritage of the Indigenous people or is it the successful exploitation of the oil, coal, water, etc. to create wealth?

This is essentially the question posed by the unique proposal brought forward by five Native American nations, Indigenous grassroots community members, and conservationists. What value does the past hold? Does it matter that antiquities and ancient sites be undisturbed? Is there more value in mining and the right to ride ATVs over thousands of archaeological sites?

And not only are 100,000 archaeological sites endangered, but so is Navajo (Diné) culture. The Navajo Nation is one of the largest Native Nations within the United States. Its land base is the size of Ireland; it   has 350,000 members—a population equal to that of Iceland; it is also larger than more than twenty member states of the United Nations. Over 125,000 Navajos speak their language fluently—the most of any Indigenous language in the United States. However, the culture depends on isolated communities like those found in San Juan County, Utah, to continue to survive.

Traditional Navajo communities and their elders have borne the brunt of energy development in the Southwest since World War II when the Navajo Nation's uranium resources were used to win the war. To this day there are hundreds of open uranium mines that have not been cleaned up, which poison the water and health of the people. At Black Mesa, coal strip mining has led to the forced removal of thousands of Navajo. Many families were "relocated" to the Puerco River, the site of the largest uranium spill in US history. The coal is transported by slurrying—a process draining precious drinking water from the Navajo-Hopi aquifer—using the only slurry line in North America. The Public Lands Initiative presented by Rep. Bishop (R-Utah) in Congress in 2016 will open up more Navajo communities to be victimized by mining.

And what value do culturally intact Navajo communities provide to America? One need only look at American history to see the huge impact that cultural exchanges between American colonists and Indigenous nations like the once-powerful Iroquois Confederacy made on the world.

It has been well-documented that it was the Iroquois that urged the thirteen colonies to unite, as the Six Nations of their confederacy had done to bring peace and stability to the region.[1] The Great Law of Peace of the Haudenosaunee (Iroquois) was also a living example of a working democratic government the colonists could see first-hand.

It is no accident that the first women's rights conference was held in Seneca Falls, New York—adjacent to a Seneca village. The

---

[1] United States. Cong. Senate. Concurrent Resolution to Acknowledge Contribution of Iroquois Confederacy to Development of US Constitution. 100th Cong. 2nd sess. H. Con. Res. 331 (1988). H. Con. Res. 331.

Seneca were one of the six nations of the Iroquois Confederacy. White women observed daily the greater rights Iroquois women enjoyed. At a time when American women were legally dead, the Iroquois Confederacy, which was matrilineal with ultimate power over the leadership held by clan mothers, was a vision of another world for European-American women.[2] This living example of a society where women had a real role and respect gave them the courage to challenge thousands of years of patriarchy that dehumanized women. In their speeches, Elizabeth Cady Stanton and Lucretia Mott exclaimed that they wanted the rights they saw Seneca women had.

In these examples one can clearly see the value of cross-cultural exchanges between the "old world" and the "new." Indigenous cultures isolated in the Americas managed to retain or to grow ideas of social organizing long lost in the rest of the world. It is no exaggeration to say these exchanges produced ideas that have made lives better for billions of people in the world today.

These original and unique cultural ideas exist in traditional Navajo communities today. The land contains not only beauty, history, and energy resources, but the cultural resources that represent human intelligence and the source of ideas that make life better in ways we cannot yet predict.

The fight for our traditional communities and cultural access to our traditional homelands and sacred sites is part of a monumental effort being conducted by Indigenous communities in a variety of ways, from exertion of sovereignty to working with federal agencies to develop co-management ideas like the Bears Ears

2 Roesch Wagner, Sally. "The Untold Story of The Iroquois Influence On Early Feminists by Sally Roesch Wagner." The Untold Story of The Iroquois Influence On Early Feminists by Sally Roesch Wagner. Feminist.com, n.d. Web. 06 Dec. 2016.

National Monument proposal. Although Bears Ears is the first unified effort of several different Indigenous nations to create a national monument and demonstrates an unusual degree of collaboration among Indigenous communities and leadership, it will not be the last.

SOME THOUGHTS ON A LONG-TERM STRATEGY FOR BEARS EARS

ANDREW CURLEY

BEARS EARS IN SOUTHERN UTAH IS A PLACE OF HISTORIC
and cultural significance. It has been home to Indigenous people for thousands of years, and continues to be an important site
for Indigenous communities, with many Navajo and Ute people
living in the region today. It is also a place of struggle, a struggle
against modern forms of colonialism that are incumbent in the
political powers of the State of Utah and the federal government
over tribes.

But tribal peoples and their governments are pushing back.
They have joined with grassroots organizations and nongovernmental organizations in an effort to have the Bears Ears
designated as a national monument.

There is intense debate about this initiative. Both Native and
non-Native residents and local and national officials are arguing about the appropriateness of this designation. Environmental
groups, non-Native conservation organizations, and tribal peoples,
have come together to petition President Obama to declare Bears
Ears a national monument.

Utah lawmakers—non-Native and staunchly conservative—along
with some local tribal members and non-Native residents are
either skeptical toward or opposed to the monument designa-

tion. Utah's congressional delegation and elected state officials want to allow for future mining and unmanaged recreation in the area and oppose the monument status as federal overreach. Some tribal residents living in the Bears Ears area fear a monument status would turn out to be an encroachment on traditional uses of the lands.

But these are not unfamiliar dynamics for tribes. Native communities in the Four Corners area are surrounded by national monuments and have used them effectively to promote infrastructure and tourism we might not otherwise afford. Most importantly, we have used these sites to gain political leverage over the land. For example, in Canyon de Chelly, a national monument inside the Navajo reservation, monument status was pursued and declared in 1930 to preserve the ancient ruins in the canyon and prevent non-Native tourists from desecrating it. Today the monument enjoys a symbiotic relationship with the tribe and the Navajo community of Chinle. It provides tourism that supports hotels and restaurants. It is vital to the Navajo tourist economy. It is not an ideal relationship, but it is better than allowing for the destruction of ancient ruins and the dominance of outside traders in tourism.

In the 1960s, the Navajo Nation Council approved federal energy projects, first a hydroelectric dam and then a coal-fired power plant, to prevent state governments from developing these energy projects over the objections of tribes. The council felt working with the Bureau of Reclamation at the time would prevent the State of Arizona from sidelining tribes.

We also leased land for a road from US Route 160 to the Navajo National Monument, one of the oldest national monuments in the park service and located in the reservation, as a way to benefit

Navajo communities in the area and promote Navajo tourism. These examples demonstrate that tribes are not unfamiliar with making agreements with federal entities and sometimes conceding authority to the federal government in order to preserve places of cultural significance or to maintain any notion of political authority over our lands.

Indigenous nationalists will disagree with any diminishment of an absolute claim over our territory. They would ask why we should agree to any collaboration with the federal government, given its history of colonialism and forced displacement. These are legitimate concerns. But we need to recognize that we lack control over these places right now. We cannot allow for the destruction of these sacred sites and archaeological places because we lack the capacity and legal authority to prevent wholesale destruction.

Leveraging the authority of the federal government over state governments is a strategy tribal leaders have used effectively for many years. With the Canyon de Chelly National Monument and the Navajo National Monument, we allowed federal management over these archaeological sites in order to preserve them for future generations. Through the authority of the federal government, we have prevented state claims and curbed the exploitive practices of non-Native traders. Ideally, we would operate these places as our own tribal parks, such as Monument Valley and Antelope Point, and for national monuments in the Navajo reservation, we should eventually request this.

However, for Bears Ears, which lies outside of the boundaries of the Navajo Nation, we should promote federal management to prevent private or state-sanctioned development that is the status quo. Non-Native settlers continue to move into the area and are eying it for expansion of energy and real estate development.

These activities would damage sacred sites, scar places of archaeological significance, and continue to marginalize Native people in their own lands. Through a national monument status, with a just co-management agreement, we might gain political authority over a region we currently don't control, even if this authority is limited.

Critics will rightly contend that co-management is not an ideal status for tribes. We are indigenous to the land and by right should have complete authority. But the political reality is that we don't. And the State of Utah will not concede any additional lands to the Navajo Nation or any other tribe, especially in areas with potential subterranean minerals or that might augment the Navajo Nation's claims to the upper Colorado River. Tribes fit within the political nexus of US federalism between the national government and state governments. We should recognize this tension between the federal and state governments and use it to our advantage.

Of course, there is a real danger that a national monument designation will make things worse for tribes. Perhaps President Obama ignores tribal requests for co-management and declares the area under complete federal control, displacing tribal people from the discussion and the area. Displacing and evicting already marginalized people from natural areas is a problem in the establishment of national parks or biological reserves throughout the world. We should guard against this danger and not allow non-Native, nongovernmental groups to dominate the conversation. Indigenous actors have the most at stake and ought to lead the effort. Another potential danger is that Obama's monument decree is too weak and allows for continued resource development and forms of recreation that are a threat to sacred sites.

In the end, the proposal to turn Bears Ears into a national monument suffers from many flaws. Tribes are forced to partner with non-Native nongovernmental organizations and non-Native settlers, developers, and state officials to determine how this area should be used. It is a tragedy of colonialism that we are in this predicament. Ideally, all the tribes who had a stake in Bears Ears would talk amongst ourselves and come up with a way to jointly use and conserve the area. But the reality of the situation is that non-Natives are free to transverse these areas, access ancient archaeological sites, and pursue environmentally destructive forms of energy development. We need to preserve these places for future generations of Indigenous peoples. We ought to learn from our ancestors, who strategically leveraged the authority of the federal government to prevent wholesale destruction and Indigenous displacement. From a national monument status, one day we might turn this land into tribal land. But we need to first check further encroachments from the State of Utah and non-Native communities in the area. This is why we should support the effort to declare the Bears Ears a national monument.

A national monument status with tribal co-management is not the ideal form of Indigenous sovereignty, but it is a step toward it.

SPIRIT OF PLACE: PRESERVING THE CULTURAL LANDSCAPE OF THE BEARS EARS

LYLE BALENQUAH

1200 A.D.

DAWN BREAKS OVER A SECLUDED CANYON, SPREADING
a sliver of orange light along the rim as a lone wren welcomes
the morning, singing another day into existence. As the light increases intensity, it works its way down a sheer cliff face, revealing
layers of geologic time: ancient cross-bedded sand dunes and the
compressed remains of million-year-old ocean floors that contain the fossilized remains of sea creatures whose descendants
now inhabit oceans and seas hundreds of miles away. The stone
façade warms into a kaleidoscope of colors—red, orange, pink, yellow, tan, brown, purple, each one blending into the other as if a
giant brush of watercolors swept across the surface. At the final
moment of reveal, the sunlight works its way to the canyon bottom where at the last precipice of stone, an alcove appears. At
first an arch of darkness, the protected interior starts to glow with
reflected light, and the details of the alcove come into view.

Inside, a cluster of structures stands, some two stories tall. Tiny
T-shaped doorways peer out into the world. Built of stone, mortar
and adobe, the protruding roof beams begin to cast long shadows
against the coursed masonry. The human occupants of this small
village, the *Hisat'sinom* ("People of Long Ago") are already beginning their day. Men collect their tools and set off to tend to fields
spread out in the canyon bottoms or to embark on hunting trips
on the mesa tops above. Women gather together, teaching their
daughters the fine art of creating intricately woven baskets and

ceramics decorated with images that depict their histories: clan lineages, epic migrations, and silent prayers for moisture. Here and there, children, turkeys, and dogs fill the spaces with their cries, laughter and energy.

This canyon is their world. A brief moment of time in which they create an understanding that is embedded in the existence of experiences. Seasons pass and the revolutions of the sun, moon and stars signal times of growth, harvest, ceremony and celebration. Old ones are laid to rest with reverence, while young ones are welcomed in to fill the voids. All the while, the people continue on in their journeys, building upon knowledge of previous ancestors, each generation adding their own energies to a collective knowledge as they face an uncertain future.

All across the area known today as the Bears Ears, this scene plays out in canyons, mesa tops, and river bottoms in thousands of similar villages. For millennia, the *Hisat'sinom*, ancestors of modern Hopi people, lived in this region, refining the practical know-how and spiritual energy that allowed them to not only exist, but thrive in a seemingly harsh environment. This knowledge and experience would be passed from generation to generation, ultimately culminating and expressed in the contemporary culture of Hopi people, reflecting a connection that spans thousands of years across hundreds of miles.

Eventually the revolutions of the earth out-distance the early *Hisat'sinom* and all that is left of their passing are their ancient homes, tools, textiles, ceramics, jewelry, and images carved and painted upon the cliff walls. In some cases, the physical remains of revered family are interred within and around the structures, left as spiritual guardians of a holy space. These are the tangible remains of their existence, ones that we can see and in some cases, touch and feel with our own hands; some are experienced in the relative comfort of museums, archives and research centers across the country. Others, if we are lucky enough, are encountered in our own wanderings across the same landscapes the Ancient Ones once called home. Under the same sun, moon, and stars they once gazed upon, we can hold in our hands the results of thousands of years of living within a natural world. For many of us, Indigenous and otherwise, we sense the sacred as we glimpse into the lives of the Ancient Ones.

Yet there is another aspect of this landscape that cannot be readily seen or touched by our human hands. This is the *Spirit of Place*. It is the quiet solitude of the evening sunset, the sudden rush of excitement watching a falcon pursue its prey across the grasslands, the overwhelming expression of humility as we gaze upon stars, planets and other celestial bodies in the dark night sky. All of these experiences are afforded us because many of the landscapes of the Bears Ears remain in a relatively pristine condition. The open space of the canyons, mesas, deserts, forests, riparian areas, streams, and rivers still connect to one another and to those wild inhabitants that call this place home. These landscapes are not broken up into islands of refuge, as is the case with so many areas due to the encroachment of human development upon the natural space.

This area holds the same spirit the *Hisat'sinom* also witnessed, compelling them to record their expressions of those experiences upon the cliff faces, conveyed through the beauty of their arts and remembered in story, song, and prayer. This is the legacy that modern Hopi descendants still carry with them. The connection to this ancestral spirit still resonates in the contemporary culture of Hopi people. It is a connection that transcends both time and space, so that as a Hopi person enacts their own ceremony, both public and private, they are recalling the hardships and accomplishments of their ancestors. The history of Hopi people is recorded upon the landscapes of their ancestors. Thus, maintaining Hopi culture is more than merely an act of writing down these events and places; it must encompass the actual preservation of those places where the ancestors dwell.

An important aspect of cultural preservation, from the Hopi perspective, requires that one be able to experience the natural settings of their ancestors, be able to journey back to those places and see first-hand how their ancestors lived. To walk among the centuries-old homes where generations lived, to hold in their hands the pieces of art created by hands of distant relatives, to sit upon towering buttes and recognize landscapes that are recalled from prayer. For modern Hopi people, our oral histories contain the memories and essence of Hopi ancestors and homelands and these histories remain viable aspects of Hopi culture.

Being able to actually experience our ancestral landscapes aids in the understanding of what a "cultural landscape" really is. In an age when Indigenous oral histories are continually challenged as viable sources of information, at least for some in academia, the need to defend our histories becomes paramount. This includes preserving not just the oral histories, but the actual, real-life sites where our ancestors lived, granting future generations of Hopi the opportunity to follow their ancestors' footprints across the landscape.

Anthropologists Ferguson and Kuwanwisiwma explain that for today's Hopi,

> *Ancestral villages that have fallen into ruin are not dead places whose only meaning comes from scientific values.*

The Hopi ancestors who lived in these villages still spiritually occupy these places, and these ancestors play an integral role in the contemporary Hopi ceremonies that bring rain, fertility, and other blessings for the Hopi people and their neighbors throughout the world. "Itaakuku" -footprints-are thus a part of the living legacy of the ancestors, and they play a vital role in the religious activities essential to the perpetuation of Hopi society.

In essence, by acknowledging our ancestors' existence, they acknowledge ours through the answering of our prayers. This understanding provides a continual connection between modern Hopi people and their forebears. This connection is contained within the landscapes, where Hopi ancestors interacted with their natural environments, leaving a legacy behind that their descendants must now strive to continue.

The Bears Ears movement is about more than just preservation for preservation's sake, more than drawing a line on a map to protect a fragile ecosystem from the development of the fossil fuel industry. It's also about more than protection of archaeological sites from wanton vandalism or preservation of these sites for solely scientific purposes. It's about the protection of Indigenous cultures so that we retain our ability to pass on our traditional knowledge to future generations. Protection of this landscape allows us to share with the outside world that we are more than historical footnotes, to show that our connections to ancestral lands traverse distance and time. Only through these continued efforts will future generations of Hopi people have their own cultural ground to stand upon, providing them the opportunity to interact with their ancestral past as we have done since time immemorial.

At the heart of this unified tribal effort is a call for *Respect*. Respect for a landscape that holds the spirit and essence of Indigenous history and culture. Imagine that it is one hundred years from the present day, at a canyon awaiting the break of day. At the rim of the canyon, a few moments before the sunlight graces the sandstone cliffs from the eastern horizon, there stands a small group of unified tribal members. They have gathered to witness the same scene experienced by those early *Hisat'sinom* families. They have gathered to pay their respects, as a lone canyon wren sings the day into existence, to offer reverence and say to their ancestors, We Are Still Here.

ON LOCKE'S "COMMONS" AND NATIVE KINSHIP WITH THE LAND

KIMBALL BIGHORSE

EVER SINCE JOHN LOCKE ASSERTED HIS LABOR THEORY
of property, or perhaps when Adam first exercised dominion over
Creation, disputes with Indigenous peoples over land rights has
served as the canary in the coal mine for western civilization's—
and by inheritance, the United States'—relationship with Mother Earth. Alienated and lifeless, once wilderness was quickened
by man's self-exertion, it suddenly and finally had value and
vigor worth fighting for. Of course, the land's original inhabitants related to Creation as kin, even parent, a fellow Being with
a spiritual existence that was both independent of human life
and that predated and even superseded it. Earth was Mother,
other animal life was kindred with our own, and we co-exist-
ed in a delicate co-dependence. Just as one's mother could not
be commoditized and bought and sold piecemeal and alienated
and adopted with the shake of a hand or the stroke of a pen, so
absurd was it to think, let alone say, that one "owned" a place to
the exclusion of all others, and that another place was "owned"
by another. The sun shone the same and the rain fell without
discriminating by "owner."

Yet here we are, with the reality of property law and "discovery"
all these centuries later, and the cause and effect that accompa-
ny them, some parties arguing for and against Bears Ears attaining national monument status because of difference of opinion

about tourism dollars lost or forfeited, freedom to traverse by motorized vehicle continued or restricted, even resources denied or allowed to be gathered for ceremonial or spiritual purposes. All this setting aside the matters of varyingly mutually exclusive federal, state, and tribal "interests."

The State of Utah argues that local folks know best, and Utah politicians advance a proposal that increases state control of sacred lands, declaring that federal bureaucrats are clueless about what should or should not be allowed, and that Indians don't need "another reservation." They say that national monument status is too broad and restrictive, when one bit of territory doesn't require the same protections another bit requires. Of course, at the heart of the issues being decided is Who Ultimately Does the Deciding. Predictably, tribal "interests" are relegated to an arguably (or not so arguably?) advisory role in Utah's plans for the Bears Ears, when really, don't we all know that the contest is between which American institutions should take the steering wheel here?

But the State's proposal ultimately feels like so much baby-halving. A bit of energy development here, a bit of artifact-preventing there, here a fence, there a fence, with a rulebook on every fence post with a punitive schedule of fees in the appendix and roads all over. Doesn't some land deserve to just be? Tribal interests might just be what the land would ask for itself if it had a voice.

Admittedly, national monument status is merely assigning Decider status over to another institution, but at least the federal apparatus realizes that some places hold "value"—whatever that means—to people outside the state's boundaries. And who can doubt that what the Grand Canyon might want for itself and what Arizona might want may not be the same thing? Or Yosemite and California? Or Zion and Utah? One can't drive directly into most of these places, one can only take a shuttle, so as to control and limit the footprint of humanity upon them. What a fantastic idea! The result is that someone from Florida or North Dakota or even Zimbabwe can behold and be inspired by the awesomeness of the landscape, or put another way, feel the kinship the Natives do that can otherwise be abstracted away by the veneer of privatization.

Finally, there is an irony at play here that can easily escape one's attention. So much of the value of Bears Ears is in the stories told by the clues left behind by the previous ancient inhabitants. The dwellings, drawings, and pot sherds sprinkled throughout the area attract looters and exploiters and arguably make Bears Ears a poster child for the stated intent of the Artifacts Act. But those artifacts represent more than just remnants: so much labor mixed with the surroundings by the ancestors of the Indigenous inhabitants that survive today, who fight so hard to give voice to the land that has supported human life since before Columbus. It's hard to say how and if he'd be welcomed, but it's also not too hard to imagine even Mr. Locke reluctantly nodding his head and standing with them in their cause. For, according to him, even "ownership" rights are subject to the proviso that "...there is enough, and as good, left in common for others."

THE SAN FRANCISCO
PEAKS AND THE POLITICS
OF CULTURAL GENOCIDE

KLEE BENALLY

THE HISTORY OF NATIVE AMERICANS IN AMERICA AFTER European contact and colonization is a history of trauma: degradation of Native American populations and cultures from disease, appropriation of and removal from traditional lands, forced disuse of native languages and native subsistence lifeways, separation of families through boarding schools and adoption, suppression of Native American religions, and out-right genocide. These actions and others by the Spanish, French, English, and, later, the Government and citizens of the United States, left a legacy of trauma that continues to plague Native American communities. We recognize that the poli-cies of self-determination and self-governance are intended to help remedy some of that harm. We also recognize that the continued existence of and access to Native American Sacred Sites is an important component to necessary healing. To disregard the value of Native American Sacred Sites would perpetuate the cycle of trauma.

USDA and Forest Service:
Draft Sacred Sites Policy Review,
Page 2

On December 6, 2012, the same day that Secretary Tom Vilsack of the US Department of Agriculture (USDA) issued his final report on sacred sites and an inter-agency memorandum to work toward sacred sites protection, the US Forest Service, which is managed by the USDA, filed federal charges against myself and three others. I was held for five hours in a federal holding cell in Flagstaff, Arizona, with my feet shackled, a chain around my waist, and my wrists handcuffed to links in that steel chain.

For our role in delivering a letter in a protest three months earlier, the four of us were being charged with "Threatening, resisting, intimidating, or interfering with any forest officer engaged in or on account of the performance of his official duties in the protection, improvement, or administration of the National Forest System."

On September 21, 2012, more than a dozen community members peacefully delivered letters at the Coconino National Forest Service office in Flagstaff to address the USDA's policy on sacred places. We were specifically addressing the Forest Service's role in permitting ski area expansion and treated sewage snowmaking on the San Francisco Peaks, a site in Northern Arizona managed as public lands and held holy since time immemorial by more than thirteen Indigenous nations.

It seemed to be no coincidence that two weeks after our arrests, the privately owned Arizona Snowbowl was set to become the first and only ski area in the world to make snow from 100% treated sewage.

Do'okoosliid, more widely known as the San Francisco Peaks, are one of six holy mountains in Diné cosmology. The Peaks represent one of four pillars that uphold our universe. They are home to deities, an offering site, and a place where we gather herbs that cannot be gathered elsewhere. They are integral to the existence and wellbeing of Diné. I grew up learning of the unique relationship that we have to this holy mountain from my father, Jones Benally, who is a recognized traditional medicine practitioner and Arizona "Living Treasure." As an extension of these teachings and ceremonial practices, a major part of my life has focused on education and building awareness of the environmental and social conflict regarding the Peaks and seeking protection of this holy place. Most conspicuously, I've helped establish the Save the Peaks Coalition, directing a feature documentary about the issue, and supporting an ongoing direct action campaign called Protect the Peaks.

In 2002, multimillionaire Snowbowl owner Eric Borowski crafted a plan to expand the ski area with new runs and lifts, and build a 14.8-mile pipeline from the City of Flagstaff to a ten million gallon storage pond to spray 180 million gallons of treated sewage effluent to make fake snow. The plan couldn't happen without support from the City of Flagstaff, so after two council meetings a decision was quickly rendered to sell treated sewage effluent to Snowbowl. The treated sewage had been found to contain pharmaceuticals, hormones, and anti-bacterial resistance genes that pose a potential risk to human health, but city officials cast off those concerns, stating that the Forest Service would determine whether or not those threats were significant. Every Indigenous voice and every person who expressed concern for the environment, public health, or animals was ignored.

In 2004, after a half-hearted Environmental Impact Statement (EIS) process, Nora Rasure, then Coconino Forest Service supervisor, approved the ski area expansion while admitting adverse cultural impacts that were "irreversible" and "irretrievable" and would "contaminate the spiritual entirety of the San Francisco

Peaks." She spoke at a meeting of elders, medicine people, and political leaders from the thirteen Indigenous nations who hold the Peaks holy. "But, you have to remember," she said, "I also have to protect the rights of the skiers." The EIS generated under her regime had stated, "Snowmaking and expansion of facilities, especially the use of reclaimed water, would contaminate the natural resources needed to perform the required ceremonies that have been, and continue to be, the basis for the cultural identity for many of these tribes" (Final Environmental Impact Statement, Vol 1: 3-18).

In the final EIS, Daniel Peaches, member of the Diné Medicine Man's Association, stated, "Once the tranquility and serenity of the Mountain is disturbed, the harmony that allows for life to exist is disrupted. The weather will misbehave, the ground will shift and tremble, the land will no longer be hospitable to life. The natural pattern of life will become erratic and the behaviors of animals and people will become unpredictable. Violence will become the norm and agitation will rule so peace and peacefulness will no longer be possible. The plants will not produce berries and droughts will be so severe as to threaten all existence" (Final Environmental Impact Statement, Vol 1: 3-27).

Joe Shirley, former president of the Navajo Nation, stated that "to Diné, the sacred mountain of the West represents life itself. Dook'o'osliid is one of our strengths. It is our essence. It is us." While in office, Shirley declared the Snowbowl expansion an "act of cultural genocide."

However, the City of Flagstaff and the Chamber of Commerce were delighted at Rasure's decision. They saw the dollars pouring into Flagstaff from dirty snow. In their minds, the marginal seasonal economic gain from a single for-profit private business outweighed the interests of thirteen Indigenous nations—and the ecological integrity of the mountain. Although the Navajo and Hopi Nations argued that they contributed more significantly to the economy of Flagstaff (a contribution that has yet to be studied) and their cultures were a significant draw for tourists from throughout the world, those realities were ignored.

Subsequent to the Forest Service decision in 2004, Indigenous nations and environmental groups filed lawsuits addressing religious freedom and environmental violations. Ultimately, the courts decided that "the only effect of the proposed upgrades is on the Plaintiffs' subjective, emotional religious experience. That is, the presence of recycled wastewater on the Peaks is offensive to the Plaintiffs' religious sensibilities...the diminishment of spiritual fulfillment—serious though it may be—is not a 'substantial burden' on the free exercise of religion." The court dismissed our religious beliefs, referring to them as "damaged spiritual feelings."

In this case, the courts, made up of all non-Natives, affirmed their anti-Indigenous bias and concluded that our deeply held beliefs are merely an "emotionally subjective experience." In the same decision, three judges filed a dissenting opinion stating that the ruling "misstates the evidence...misstates the law under the [Religious Freedom Restoration Act], and misunderstands the very nature of religion."

In 2009, when the Supreme Court denied a petition appealing the ruling, Howard Shanker, the attorney representing the Navajo Nation, Havasupai Tribe, White Mountain Apache Nation, Yavapai-Apache Nation, and three environmental groups, argued that "in a country that supposedly values the free exercise and accommodation of all religion, it is unconscionable that Native American religious and cultural beliefs have essentially been relegated to second-class status by the federal government."

Of course, part of the message in the dominant culture is that as long as Indigenous cultures are safely on a shelf, in a book, in a museum, or in the form of entertainment, they are valid, accepted, and celebrated. This dynamic exists at the nexus of racism and capitalism. This is not surprising in Arizona, a state that legislatively suppresses cultural education and promotes racial profiling.

In September 2009, the Save the Peaks Coalition and nine plaintiffs filed a new lawsuit addressing the 2005 Forest Service decision approving artificial snowmaking at Snowbowl. The suit asserted that the Forest Service failed to conduct a thorough analysis if humans were to ingest snow made from treated sewage, but this was ruled against in the Ninth Circuit in 2012.

The USDA initiated listening sessions in 2010 to address policy issues with sacred places. The draft policy review stated, "The Forest Service is committed to restoring our forests and the vital resources important to our survival, while wisely respecting the need for a natural resource economy that creates jobs and vibrant rural communities. Respecting, honoring, accommodating, and protecting Native American Sacred Sites must be part of that commitment" (USDA and Forest Service: Draft Sacred Sites Policy Review: 3). In the midst of the comment period for input on the draft policy, the USDA gave the green light to Snowbowl to desecrate the Holy Peaks.

In 2011, after years of legal battles—including the Save the Peaks Coalition suit still under judicial review—Snowbowl started clear-cutting seventy-four acres of rare alpine habitat for new runs and lifts and constructing a 14.8-mile buried pipeline to transport treated sewage to make artificial snow on 205 acres.

On June 16, 2011, six land defenders chained themselves to heavy machinery desecrating the Holy Peaks. They issued the following statement:

PROTECT THE PEAKS – STOP DESTRUCTION & DESECRATION NOW!

Today we take direct action to stop further desecration and destruction of the Holy San Francisco Peaks. We stand with our ancestors, with allies and with those who also choose to embrace diverse tactics to safeguard Indigenous People's cultural survival, our community's health, and this sensitive mountain ecosystem.

On May 25th, 2011, sanctioned by the US Forest Service, owners of Arizona Snowbowl began further destruction and desecration of the Holy San Francisco Peaks. Snowbowl's hired work crews have laid over a mile and a half of the planned 14.8-mile wastewater pipeline. They have cut a six-foot wide and six-foot deep gash into the Holy Mountain.

Although a current legal battle is under appeal, Snowbowl owners have chosen to undermine judicial process by rushing to construct the pipeline. Not only do they disregard culture, environment, and our children's health, they have proven that they are criminals beyond reproach.

Four weeks of desecration has already occurred. Too much has already been taken. Today, tomorrow and for a healthy future, we say "enough!"

As we take action, we look to the East and see Bear Butte facing desecration, Mt. Taylor facing further uranium

---

mining; to the South, Mt. Graham desecrated, South Mountain threatened, the US/Mexico border severing Indigenous communities from sacred places; to the West, inspiring resistance at Sogorea Te, Moana Keya facing desecration; to the North, Mt. Tenabo, Grand Canyon, Black Mesa, and so many more...our homelands and our culture under assault.

We thought that the USDA, heads of the Forest Service, had meant it when they initiated nationwide listening sessions to protect sacred places. If the process was meaningful, we would not have to take action today. More than 13 Indigenous nations hold the peaks holy. The question has been asked, yet we hear no response: "What part of sacred don't you understand?"

For hundreds of years, resistance to colonialism, slavery, and destruction of Mother Earth has existed and continues here in what we now call Arizona.

The United States recently moved to join the United Nations Declaration on the Rights of Indigenous Peoples, evidently the US has not currently observed and acted upon this declaration, otherwise we would not be taking action today. This document informs our action. We also assert that UNDRIP supports the basis for our action.

"Article 11, 1: Indigenous peoples have the right to practice and revitalize their cultural traditions and customs. This includes the right to maintain, protect and develop the past, present and future manifestations of their cultures, such as archaeological and historical sites, artifacts, designs, ceremonies, technologies and visual and performing arts and literature."

"Article 11, 2: States shall provide redress through effective mechanisms, which may include restitution, developed in conjunction with indigenous peoples, with respect to their cultural, intellectual, religious and spiritual property taken without their free, prior and informed consent or in violation of their laws, traditions and customs."

"Article 12, 1: Indigenous peoples have the right to manifest, practice, develop and teach their spiritual and religious traditions, customs and ceremonies; the right to maintain, protect, and have access in privacy to their religious and cultural sites; the right to the use and control of their ceremonial objects; and the right to the repatriation of their human remains."

"Article 25: Indigenous peoples have the right to maintain and strengthen their distinctive spiritual relationship with their traditionally owned or otherwise occupied and used lands, territories, waters and coastal seas and other resources and to uphold their responsibilities to future generations in this regard."

For nearly four decades, resistance to desecration and destruction of the Peaks has been sustained. Prayer vigils, petitions, lobbying, protests, and many diverse tactics have been embraced. Historic court battles have been fought.

We continue today resisting Snowbowl's plan to spray millions of gallons of wastewater snow, which is filled with cancer-causing and other harmful contaminants, as well as to clear-cut over 30,000 trees. The Peaks are a pristine and beautiful place, a fragile ecosystem, and home to rare and endangered species of plants and animals.

Our action is a prayer.

We invite those of you who could not join us today and who believe in the protection of culture, the environment and community health to resist destruction and desecration of the Peaks:

- Join us and others in physically stopping all Snowbowl development!

- Honor and defend Indigenous Peoples' inherent right to protect Sacred Places

- Resist colonialism and capitalism! Embrace diverse tactics to end Snowbowl and all corporate greed

- Demand USDA and Snowbowl's Special Use Permit

- Demand that the City of Flagstaff Mayor and Council find a way out of their contract to sell wastewater to Snowbowl

- Demand that Arizona Department of Environmental Quality change its permission allowing wastewater to be used for snowmaking.

PROTECT THE PEAKS!

Since 2011, nearly forty arrests have been made resulting from interventions to protect the Holy Peaks from desecration.

The struggle to protect sacred places has become contentious enough that in 2011 the United Nations Special Rapporteur on the Rights of Indigenous Peoples recommended that the "United States Government engage in a comprehensive review of its relevant policies and actions to ensure that they are in compliance with international standards in relation to the San Francisco Peaks and other Native American sacred sites, and that it take appropriate remedial actions."

When it comes to protecting sacred places, Indigenous peoples have little recourse in the US legal context. The National Environmental Policy Act proves inconsistent even when traditional cultural property designations are factored in Environmental Impact Statements. For example, the Washoe Nation partnered successfully with the USFS to ban rock-climbing activities desecrating a sacred site, yet the same agency has worked against Indigenous interests in protecting areas such as the San Francisco Peaks and Mount Graham in southern Arizona. Court cases such as *Lyng v. Northwest Indian Cemetery Protective Association*, *Wilson v. Bloc*, and *Navajo Nation v US Forest Service*, clearly demonstrate that no legal mechanism exists—not the American Indian Religious Freedom Act, not the Religious Freedom Restoration Act, or the US Constitution—for protection for sacred lands. Litigation remains a tenuous and potentially disastrous option, in that negative precedence can inform judicial decisions in other cases regarding sacred land conflicts.

Developers operating on public lands have in some cases offered "buyouts." Snowbowl owners, who don't own the ski area lands but own the facilities and have the opportunity to hold the Special Use Permit issued by the USFS, offered to sell the ski facilities to the Navajo Nation for $52 million in 2010. By comparison, Snowbowl had purchased the ski area in 1992 for only $4 million. Indigenous Peoples categorically rejected the offer, recognizing that it would amount to paying ransom to developers for threatening sacred lands and further support a market for such threats.

Inconsistent application of NEPA by land management agencies and no existing laws guaranteeing protection of Indigenous Peoples' sacred places place Indigenous lifeways in constant peril. Indigenous Peoples are forced to seek creative solutions to gain whatever protections available, such as the national monument designations sought by the Bears Ears Inter-Tribal Coalition and by the San Carlos Apache Nation for Oak Flat near Globe, Arizona. While these designations would certainly be welcome, they may only provide indirect relief from violations of free exercise of religion in relation to sacred places, and will have impact limited to the specific sacred sites under threat.

When domestic options have been exhausted, Indigenous nations have been compelled to seek audience on the international level. On March 2, 2015, the Navajo Nation filed a complaint against the United States with the Inter-American Commission on Human Rights, alleging violations of the Navajo people's rights to practice their religion and culture regarding desecration of the San Francisco Peaks. Yet even the lawyer who filed the complaint on the Navajo Nation's behalf is not very optimistic. "No government ever changes its policy because an international body says to," says Robert Williams, who is also professor of law and faculty co-chair of the University of Arizona's Indigenous Peoples Law and Policy program. "The Navajo know very well that the US doesn't have to listen to the report, but we hope that it feels obligated to change its conduct."

How can it be that today, Indigenous Peoples have no guaranteed protection for religious freedom when it comes to public land management decisions? This is a grave hypocrisy for a nation that was established by immigrants seeking refuge from religious persecution.

From the holy San Francisco Peaks to Bears Ears and beyond, a history of unjust mismanagement and misuse is scarred into sacred landscapes throughout the Southwest. Characterized and whitewashed through Hollywood movies and history books, Indigenous Peoples have been violently railroaded by dominant culture throughout the expansion of the "American frontier." Today the edifice of western civilization is still being carved out of and through sacred lands, with acts of desecration that perpetuate spiritual invasion, occupation, and conquest. Sacred places are the front lines in the fight for Indigenous Peoples' cultural existence. They are also in the targets of individuals and corporations who see Mother Earth as not a living entity but only as a resource that can be exploited for material gain. Every sacred site that is currently being threatened with desecration faces the menace of some form of resource extraction. Whether it's coal beneath Black Mesa, gold at Mt. Tenabo, copper under Oak Flat, oil in the Arctic National Wildlife Refuge, natural gas at Chaco Canyon, uranium at Red Butte and Mt. Taylor, geothermal at Medicine Lake, telescopes on Mount Graham or Mauna Kea, or recreation at the San Francisco Peaks, these are all forms of resource extraction that are a direct result of the commodification of our natural environment. From Mother Earth to our bodies, everything has been reduced to a commodity. Nothing is sacred in the context of capitalism. So long as Mother Earth is reduced to a commodity we will have this conflict.

As protests against ski area expansion and treated sewage snowmaking waged on, we were able to summarize our struggle in the question, "What part of sacred don't you understand?" In other words, why isn't it enough for Indigenous Peoples to state that a place is sacred and should be respected? Why should we be forced to justify our legitimate deeply held beliefs in terms that are not our own?

To desecrate a sacred place it has to be stripped of living cultural meaning and relations. This process cannot easily occur while Indigenous belief systems exist, because people tend to fight back when their ways of life are threatened. When outright killing, forced removal or relocation is not politically or publicly palatable, the first act of desecration is erasure of identity, cultural memory and relation to land. This invisibilization occurs through the systematic delegitimization of deeply held Indigenous belief systems and is an expression of white supremacy. The political strategy has also been employed through non-recognition of Indigenous nations, ensuring their relationships to sacred land bases are not fully honored.

These are vital understandings that place Indigenous lifeways in direct conflict with this capitalist system that has been violently established through colonial conquest. We are of this earth, and so where there is a crisis of the environment there is also a cultural crisis.

When I would travel by the western side of Doko'o'osliid with my clan grandmother and Big Mountain relocation and coal mining resistor Roberta Blackgoat, she would speak of Arizona Snowbowl's desecration in these terms: "The ski runs are scars on our mother; she needs to heal." The Peaks are understood as a living entity.

This understanding is what Amanda Lickers, from the Seneca Nation, identifies as *land trauma*. Lickers offers this definition:

The embodied feelings of breeched consent on our lands and bodies. The emotional and spiritual suffering experienced by Indigenous peoples as a result of physical attacks on our lands and waters [speaking] to the emotional and spiritual experiences of loss of land and identity. This also includes feelings of loss as we witness other living relations suffer or disappear as a result of these attacks, such as buffalo, wild rice, salmon, etc. Land trauma can also refer to feelings of grief and pain that have been inferred or absorbed through our lands and waters. Land trauma is different for each person as our Nations have different histories of contamination and displacement and the severity can vary depending on what part of our heritage/identity has been violated (i.e. desecration of an origin place).

In sacred places, desecration is land trauma. On the Peaks, the trauma is exacted at the point of destruction with clear cuts and pipeline trenches, and held in the contaminated herbs and medicines, the polluted springs, the unsuspecting animals who drink the water, and in the overall eco/spiritual-system that is part of the lifeline that is a foundation of who we are as Indigenous Peoples. The trauma extends through our social/cultural relations and directly interferes with the effectiveness of our prayers and ceremonies. It intervenes with the physical relationship that we maintain and impacts our ability to heal our bodies. The hetero-patriarchal underpinning of colonialism ensures that Indigenous women and two-spirit people are disproportionately targeted by violence of desecration.

As Amanda Lickers further illustrates, "if you're destroying and poisoning the things that give us life, the things that shape our identity, the places that we are from and the things that sustain us, then how can you not be poisoning us? How can that not be direct violence against our bodies, whether that be respiratory illness or cancer or liver failure, or the inability to carry children."

The NEPA process offers no meaningful mechanism to quantify these social impacts and their compound effects; sacred places are connected through complex spiritual systems; when one is desecrated and then another, the effects are compounded. Until those who benefit from the systems that are entangled with the exploitation of Mother Earth truly understand that mountains, rivers, lakes, trees, plants, and rocks suffer the same way we do, we may only continue to ensure that the trauma is mutually assured. In this way, the defense of lands held holy by Indigenous Peoples are the frontlines in the struggles for our whole existence. If we desire to exist, we must continue to defend the sacred and liberate Mother Earth.

As I stood in chains before the federal judge on December 6, 2012, the prosecutor repeatedly requested that myself and others facing charges be "banned" from going on the San Francisco Peaks and to any Coconino Forest Service building as a condition of our release. The federal prosecutor stated that he was concerned about the possibility of further protests. Attorney Matthew Brown argued that my religious practice was directly connected to the San Francisco Peaks and restricting my access to the Holy Mountain would be akin to preventing me from going to church. The judge agreed not to ban me from the Peaks but cautioned that if I broke any laws I faced immediate imprisonment until trial. We ended up being coerced into accepting a plea deal over the charges, but the political attack served to criminalize the work that we are doing to protect the sacred mountain.

Outside the courthouse, my aunt Louise Benally, who has been resisting forced relocation from Big Mountain and coal mine desecration of Black Mesa, reminded us of a truth larger than the court's decision. "The natural laws and the Indigenous People were already here in a good relationship before the coming of the colonial society who draws laws and boundaries. However, we Indigenous Peoples will always have ties with these lands. We will continue to live that way with nature and we will carry on."

A BIRTHDAY POEM

LUCI TAPAHONSO

This morning, the sunrise is a brilliant song
cradling tiny birds and brittle leaves. The world
responds, stretching, humming. The sunlight is Diyin,
sacred beams of the Holy Ones arrive with prayers.
They bring gifts in the cold dawn. Again, as a Diné
woman, I face east on the porch and pray for Hózhó

one more time. For today, all me to share Hózhó,
the beauty of all things being right and proper as in songs
the Holy Ones gave us. They created the world,
instilling stories and lessons so we would know Diyin
surrounds us. Our lives were set by precise prayers
and stories to ensure balance. Grant me the humor Diné

elders relish so. No matter what, let the Diné
love of jokes, stories and laughter create some Hózhó.
Some days, even after great coffee, I need to hear a song
to reassure me that the distance from Dinétah is not a world
away. I know the soft hills, plains, and wind are Diyin
also. Yet I plan the next trip when we will say prayers

in the dim driveway. As we drive, Kansas darkens. Prayers
and memories protect us. In the tradition of Diné
travel, we eat, laugh, refuel, sing. Twice in Texas, Hózhó
arose in clear air above the flatness. The full moon was a song
we watched all night. After midnight, Lori asks about the Diyin

Diné'é who dance in the Night Way ceremony. The sacred Diyin
Diné'é come after the first frost glistens. Their prayers
and long rhythmic songs help us live. This is a Diné
way of communion and cleansing. At the Night Way, Hózhó
awaits as we come to listen and absorb the songs
until they live within. It is true that the world

is restored by the Holy Ones who return to the Fourth World
to take part in the Night Wway. They want to know the Diyin
still exists amongst their children. Their stories and prayers
guide us now. At times, the Holy Ones feared the Diné
would succomb to foreign ways. For them, it is truly Hózhó
to see us at the Night Way gathered in the smoky cold. Songs

rise with fire smoke. I tell Lori we Diné are made of prayers.
At times, the world may overwhelm us, yet because of the Diyin,
each morning we pray to restore Hózhó, Hózhó, Hózhó, Hózhó.

IN OUR USUAL AND ACCUSTOMED PLACES

/ INDIGENOUS LEADERS
ON BEARS EARS AND THE FIGHT
FOR CULTURAL PRESERVATION
AND ACCESS TO PUBLIC LANDS IN THE
UNITED STATES

WE WERE THE LAND'S
BEFORE WE WERE

HEID E. ERDRICH

GUIDELINES FOR THE TREATMENT OF SACRED OBJECTS

If the objects emit music,
and are made of clay or turtle shell,
bathe them in mud at rainy season.
Allow to dry, then brush clean
using only red cloth or newspaper.
Play musical objects from time to time.
Avoid stereotypical tom-tom beat
and under no circumstances dance or sway.

If objects were worn as funerary ornament,
admire them verbally from time to time.
Brass bells should be called *shiny*
rather than *pretty*. Shell ear spools
should be remarked upon as *handsome*,
but beads of all kinds can be told,
simply, that they are *lookin' good*.

Guidelines for the treatment of sacred objects
composed of wood, hair (human or otherwise)
and/or horn, include: offering smoke,
water, pollen, cornmeal or, in some instances,

honey, chewing gum, tarpaper
and tax incentives.

If an object's use is obscure,
or of pleasing avian verisimilitude,
place rocks from its place of origin
within its display case. Blue-ish rocks
often bring about discovery, black rocks
soothe or mute, while white rocks irritate mildly.
All rocks must return to their place of origin
whenever they wish. Use only volunteer rocks,
or stones left by matri-descendent patri-tribalists.

Guidelines for the treatment of sacred objects
that appear or disappear at will
or that appear larger in rear view mirrors,
include calling in spiritual leaders such as librarians,
wellness-circuit speakers and financial aide officers.

If an object calls for its mother,
boil water and immediately swaddle it.
If an object calls for other family members,
or calls collect after midnight, refer to tribally
specific guidelines. Reverse charges.

If objects appear to be human bone,
make certain to have all visitors stroke
or touch their fingertips to tibia, fibula
and pelvis fragments. In the case of skulls,
call low into the ear or eyeholes, with words
lulling and kind.

If the bones seem to mock you
or of if they vibrate or hiss,
make certain no mirrors hang nearby.
Never, at any time, sing Dem Bones.

Avoid using the bones as drumsticks
or paperweights, no matter
the actions of previous Directors or Vice
Directors of your institution.

If bones complain for weeks at a time,
roll about moaning, or leave chalky outlines,
return them instantly to their place of origin,
no questions asked. C.O.D.

THE THEFT OUTRIGHT

after Frost

We were the land's before we were.

Or the land was ours before you were a land.
Or this land was our land, it was not your land.

We were the land before we were people,
loamy roamers rising, so the stories go,
or formed of clay, spit into with breath reeking soul—

What's America, but the legend of Rock 'n' Roll?

Red rocks, blood clots bearing boys, blood sands
swimming being from women's hands, we originate,
originally, spontaneous as hemorrhage.

Un-possessing of what we still are possessed by,
possessed by what we now no more possess.

We were the land before we were people,
dreamy sunbeams where sun don't shine, so the stories go,
or pulled up a hole, clawing past ants and roots—

Dineh in documentaries scoff DNA evidence off.
They landed late, but canyons spoke them home.
Nomadic Turkish horse tribes they don't know.

What's America, but the legend of Stop 'n' Go?

Could be cousins, left on the land bridge,
contrary to popular belief, that was a two-way toll.
In any case we'd claim them, give them some place to stay.

Such as we were we gave most things outright
(the deed of the theft was many deeds and leases and claim stakes
and tenure disputes and moved plat markers stolen still today . . .)

We were the land before we were a people,
earthdivers, her darling mudpuppies, so the stories go,
or emerging, fully forming from flesh of earth—

The land, not the least vaguely, realizing in all four directions,
still storied, art-filled, fully enhanced.
Such as she is, such as she wills us to become.

IN OUR USUAL AND ACCUSTOMED PLACES

MORNING STAR GALI

"Medicine Lake is our church. It is there we heal our bodies and our spirits. Would you want a power plant in your church?"

CECELIA SILVAS, Ilmawi Band Elder

THE SACRED MEDICINE LAKE HIGHLANDS, LOCATED within a volcanic crater in Northeastern California, are known to my people, the Pit River Nation, as Sah-tit-lah—obsidian knife lake. Medicine Lake Highlands is part of the Cascade Range and is located in Northern California, northeast of Mount Shasta and south of Klamath Falls. Our elders share that the lake and surrounding area is sacred in its entirety. How can we cut out a piece of our mother's womb and dare claim that a designated portion of the lake is sacred, and a sacrificial area is not as sacred as the rest of the water body and land?

The concept of it is completely abstract to our value system, yet this is what the Department of the Interior has attempted to force on our people and surrounding tribes for almost four decades now, as we continually fight plans to build geothermal power plants in the area. In an ongoing battle to protect the highlands from Bureau of Land Management-issued licenses for geothermal hydro-fracking, the Pit River People and Native Coalition of surrounding tribes have demonstrated, held public awareness campaigns, and engaged in legal action against the US Forest Service and Bureau of Land Management.

One of the most infamous nearby landmarks is the Lava Beds (now a national monument), where Captain Jack and fifty-four Modoc warriors were among the one-hundred-fifty tribal peoples that held off over one thousand US soldiers during 1872-1873. Fifty-three US soldiers and five Modoc warriors were counted in the fatalities at the end of the six-month period. On November 29, 1904, the Modoc Forest Reserve was established. In 1907, the Modoc Forest Reserve was converted to the US Forest Service under the Transfer Act of 1905. Co-management of the Sacred Medicine Lake Highlands by the BLM and Shasta-Trinity and Modoc National Forests was established.

Medicine Lake is not only sacred to the eleven autonomous bands of the Ajumawi-Atsugewi peoples that compose the Pit River Tribe, but also to the Modoc, Karuk, Wintun, Klamath, and Shasta surrounding nations. Archaeological evidence supports over ten thousand years of continued use; however, our elders pass down the ancestral knowledge that sacred places such as Medicine Lake have been utilized since time immemorial. When asked about the relationship to Medicine Lake, our elders will express it is a spiritual one. As my auntie explains, "Now that goes back since time immemorial. It's always been Medicine Lake and the history of it is that we've all utilized it, all the tribes around close by here, I'd say in a five hundred-mile radius of Mt. Shasta. We've used the whole entire [place], and the lake is really important because people come there to swim to get themselves well. And it's always been there. Of course, now it's different. It's different but we still try to utilize it and it's not the same. Before, you could use it like a power spot. It is a power spot! And you could get strength, mental, physical and spiritual strength, just out there if you went once a year, you know, but a lot of people came and camped and utilized it repeatedly until they did get what they were looking for. But it is a spiritual place, it is a medicine place."

Our elders have shared that when *Hayweseeus* was creating the world, the maker actually swam in the lake, and left many healing properties there for the people to receive. That's really back, back to the beginning of time, beginning of everything, when the animal people were singing their songs, conducting their dances. Over ten years ago, we were told by elders that the lake is getting warmer in temperature.

On July 20, 2015, we won an important legal victory when the Ninth Circuit Court of Appeals ruled in our favor, that we had the right to challenge twenty-six of the land leases that the US Bureau of Land Management (BLM) had provided to the Calpine Corporation, without tribal consultation. These leases had effectively given authority to Calpine Energy Corporation to conduct test drilling and research geothermal development in the sacred Medicine Lake Highlands with a proposed 480-megawatt power plant project. The leases were continued for forty years without the appropriate environmental review and, again, without tribal consultation.

Calpine plans to use hydraulic fracturing chemicals to drill three kilometers, but environmental assessments have determined that geothermal mining in the Medicine Lake region will result in the release of toxins, such as hydrogen sulfide, arsenic, mercury, and other carcinogens, into the environment. These toxins have the potential to result in adverse health outcomes, such as kidney damage and cancer, to people exposed. The Indigenous people who continuously return to the area for religious, cultural, and ceremonial purposes will have disproportionate levels of exposure.

A recent study referenced as The Curry Report states that seeping snowmelt percolates for twenty to forty years beneath Medicine

Lake before emerging out of Fall River Springs, which is the third-largest spring in the world. In 1999, the Keeper of the National Register formally recognized as eligible for the National Register twenty-one interconnected sites located both in and near the Medicine Lake caldera as the Medicine Lake Area Traditional Cultural Places District.

The Pit River Nation and other affected Indigenous peoples were not consulted in the siting of the geothermal projects, nor have we given our free and informed consent to such geothermal development in the sacred Medicine Lake Highlands. Since 1996, the US Forest Service and BLM have illegally leased sixty-six square miles in the Medicine Lake Highlands to geothermal corporations and have approved geothermal development in the area.

On April 19, 2016, Judge John Mendez ruled in our favor, agreeing with what we have argued all along—that the BLM illegally extended twenty-six geothermal leases to Calpine Corporation without any tribal consultation or environmental review. "There's language in there that they'll argue makes the lease extensions mandatory rather than discretionary," points out Debbie Sivas, an environmental attorney representing the Pit River Tribe. "Of course, they would have had to do all the NEPA and NHPA work back in 1998 if they followed the law, but they're hoping to benefit from twenty years of getting away with illegally leasing the land."

Every year, more than one million acre-feet of water flows from the headlands down the Pit River to Shasta Lake, providing irrigation for farmland in California's desert-dry Central Valley. Water from the headlands flows into the Pit River, Shasta Lake Dam, Sacramento River, Bay Delta, and continues to the San Francisco Bay estuaries connected to the Pacific Ocean. A contamination of the headwaters has potential to pollute our connected waterways, which doesn't just threaten Pit River peoples and surrounding tribes, but the entire Northern California population.

Present-day human rights violations against Native peoples threaten the health and religious rights of these communities. Native nations, sacred sites coalitions, state agencies, and federal governmental entities such as the BLM and USFS all are key in conversations about sacred site protection. Sacred site protection efforts are key in protecting all people, how we care for our places of prayer and worship, areas that our ancestors used and our children continue to use, and are a reflection of caring for ourselves and our personal and collective health.

I asked my auntie about Calpine's claim that they have a good long history in working with Native people, in helping them, in protecting the land.

"Well I don't believe that drilling on a sacred mountain, in a sacred site, is helping the Indigenous people at all," she told me. "All I can see is that in the long run—and it's not going to be that long a run either—they're hurting everything and all of us. And there is no way that they can say they have a history of helping Indigenous people. That does not help us. Our sacred places are the only thing that will help us against this insurmountable government and all their rules and regulations."

CREATING A ROAD MAP OF REVERENCE

INTERVIEW WITH FAITH SPOTTED EAGLE
BY JACQUELINE KEELER

WHEN YOU ASK ME ABOUT MY WORK, I THINK IT'S NOT work but it's just a way of living. So, I don't consider it work. I just see whenever something needs to be done. It's kind of like the old traditional society that existed because things have to get done. When an issue comes up in the community, I look around and I think why isn't somebody doing something? Oftentimes there will be someone who steps up, and that's when I need to learn as an elder to wait to see if a young person is willing to do that, and to support them because it is their turn and their time.

That's essentially what I've done throughout my life. It's the way things were done in the old camp circle where the least you could do was help your people, so that is what I have done throughout my life. Within the last twenty years, I've really concentrated on looking at the importance of preserving sacred sites and ceremonial places because I grew up in those places, and I know they created a road map of reverence and a sense of meaning—of the earth and of existence—for me. And this road map of the natural world made perfect sense to me. When I see all of that perfect sense being destroyed simply for the sake of capitalism and short-term economic gain for a few? It's a travesty.

A friend of mine the other night asked me, "When did you become aware of the attack upon the Earth?" And I remembered when a friend of mine told me about Rachel Carson and her book *Silent Spring* back in the 1960s. That book really affirmed the fear that my father (Henry Spotted Eagle) had about what people were doing to the Earth. That book made such a difference in my life and I became aware that there were people other than Native people that cared about the Earth.

Many times in my life, we have had to stand up as a relative of Mother Earth and for our other relatives—the other Oceti Sakowin (Dakota-Lakota-Nakota) and other nations and, of course, family and the relatives that can't speak: the four-legged. The last time was the Keystone XL pipeline fight and we began standing forth on that in 2007. The immediate threat to the water is now the Dakota Access pipeline. As you do this interview today—which is what, July 26th?—the Army Corps of Engineers just announced that they granted a permit to Dakota Access to begin construction, and the Corps was the last agency that was holding out on the permit, the nationwide permit. So, we received some devastating news today that they have approved the permit and they have not even consulted with many of the nations within the Oceti Sakowin.

So once again, when you ask that question, "When did you start standing up?", the fact is, we never have stopped standing up because there's always a list of one hundred. I always talk about that list of one hundred, meaning that every one of those things on that list of one hundred are crucial to the well-being of our children and families and somebody has to stand up for it. I think that in the old days the camp circle took care of those things. Nowadays, we rely on federal grants and money and so, resources are not always there. And that's where the grassroots come in because we do what we have to do whether we have money or not.

But that's kind of a lead-in to what we're talking about—I don't know how much you want me to expand into KXL but we got a live one right now with the Dakota Access. Yankton is hosting a strategy meeting on Thursday at Fort Randall Casino for figuring out how we unify with this latest thing that we have been dreading: that the Corps has issued a nationwide permit with Dakota Access. The travesty about that, of course, is that it is attacking the first medicine, which is our water, and the second thing is, it is such a hypocritical move to use the name of pipeline that is called Dakota. Dakota is our word, it's our name, it's our spirit, and it's who we are. And they have the nerve to call a pipeline Dakota Access. It's just an example of settler-colonialism to the max and I just, it just completely irritates me that they would do something like that, but that's just the top of the pile there. And so we're going to have to figure out what we're going to need to do to stop this from happening.

We have to deal with a myriad of federal laws like the National Environmental Policy Act (NEPA) and National Historic Preservation Act (NHPA). Of course, it's a puzzle and it is a puzzle that doesn't fit very well together. For example, they segment jurisdiction and responsibility over a pipeline going through our traditional territories and the players involved, these federal agencies, are only responsible for an eleven-mile or a twenty-mile section the pipeline will impact. And down the road, when that pipeline breaks, the big picture doesn't matter because they are only worried about their eleven or twenty miles. This kind of thinking is insane and it is all in the name of capitalism and reflects the dynamics of settler-colonialism still at work in our homelands after hundreds of years. That's what we're dealing with right now. But in the process of fighting these fights, the most powerful thing that we will continue to fight with will be prayer—prayer, ceremonies, and spirituality.

I had the honor of working with the Walker River Paiute in Nevada and spent part of last week working with their youth. While I was there I thought, I know the Walker River Paiute—why do they sound so familiar? Then I realized that I was in the land of Wovoka, the spiritual person who brought the Ghost Dance to our people in the 1800s when the government was killing all of us, and I thought, I have to go to his grave. And so after the workshop was done, the tribal chairman of the Walker River Paiute took me to Wovoka's grave and I had a chance to pray, sing, offer tobacco. And I just stood there... I was just completely overwhelmed to think this individual on this Earth who was buried right before me had this vision and this dream to go north and to help our people and to do the Ghost Dance. And so I prayed to him and I thanked him.

And then, after I was done, I was talking to the chairman and I asked him, what did your people think of this dream? And he said, well, they are still ghost dancing and, there's a family that are descendants here and they still ghost dance and they just had their dance last month. And I said, I need to come out here and pray with them. The reason I bring that up in regard to sacred sites, is because when I went home and I was talking to one of my relatives, they said, I guess the dream didn't come true, and I said, you know, I don't think we can say that, because we're just mere human beings and we don't know how long these prayers go into the future. And in my mind, I think those Ghost Dance prayers are still going to come true. It's only been a little over a hundred years, and in the timeline of Mother Earth we measure it in even thousands of years. So, I think the prayers are still traveling and I haven't given up hope on them. When I offered those prayers to Wovoka, I said, you know we're still carrying your prayers, so it's still going to help. And so we'll continue to do that and when we have our meeting on Thursday of course that's what we're going to do first—we're going to send our prayers and the spirits moving and we will do what we have to do. It might come to fruition in a month, a year, ten years, a hundred years, but we have to believe.

When you look in terms of our extreme reverence and respect of sacred sites, I think it is inherently based on the DNA in our spirits. This is how we know this is realistic knowledge, and by protecting these sacred sites and knowing the experiences and the intricate relationships that exist, you can predict what will occur. Because when you deal with people who are indigenous to a place, which is what we are, we are talking about thousand-year-old wisdom about this land. Our relatives talk about the power of place because that power of place—it's a memory, a history, it's a guide, and it can eventually predict our future. And so, in our culture, we know that we have these prophecies and these prophecies are tied to not only the power of place, but the experience of living in certain places where we have observed natural phenomena that happen over and over again, and you can't help but learn from it.

But in a scientific world, it has to be measured; we come from two different realities, but with the environmental movement and many of the activists that I've come across, they now have the realization that there are limited resources in the natural world. I remember going to a meeting with an activist from Vancouver, BC, and we were at this Holiday Inn Express and they were expanding it and making it bigger, better, and more expensive, and she looked at it and said, how in the world is all of this infrastructure going to possibly be supported by Mother Earth? And I thought, such a simple statement, looking at the hotel building going on—and it's happening everywhere—and how in the world, with the limited resources we have on the Earth, are we going to fill this insatiable need to develop and grow and grow and grow and devour?

It reminds me of, in our tribal culture, a being we have called Eya—you probably have heard of Eya. Eya was the devourer who was like a giant that walked across the Plains and he was feared. They said that he was insatiable and he never had enough to eat and he was always devouring camps, so they would always say, "watch for Eya." There's always an Eya somewhere. And symbolically that's what the corporations are. They're devouring everything in sight.

So, I think one of the good things that have come about from the activism, the movement that grew to fight the Keystone XL pipeline, is that we work—we're standing along with relatives from what we call the Ska Oyate, the white world, and other races that realize that resources are limited and that the driving need to control nature is not necessary, that personal and ethical responsibility to the natural world is going to save our grandchildren, and that's what we have to do.

I remember my father saying something in the 1970s. I think it was after I told him about Rachel Carson's writing and he was telling me, he said, you know, when the Euro-American people came to the United States they didn't have too much body memory of being on this continent. He said, as the years go by, and as they bury more relatives on this Turtle Island [continent], their spirits are going to have a memory of this place, and they are going to become more and more what we call indigenous now. And I think that's happening because they have relatives buried here. So, I think the younger generation that is coming up has an attachment to this land, finally. They are still small in numbers but I have hope that that will grow.

I remember one of the meetings that we sat in. There were twenty white farmers and ranchers and landowners that were sitting on a panel at the meeting, and they were moved to tears. They were crying because they were losing their land and we were sitting there watching them because we were very familiar with losing our land. Then, somebody in the audience said, "You're like the new Indians, you know what it feels like now to lose land." And so, we were able to identify common ground. That could not occur until they had that sense of powerlessness—that there was absolutely nothing they could do to stop the pipeline—and this is happening again with the Dakota Access pipeline.

I realized that a lot of people are too afraid or too mired in poverty to do anything about it. If you think of it, some of the farmers that are close to these transmission lines are in debt—probably for the rest of their life. If you buy big machinery, that's an awful lot of money, so they really are tied to the land. But I would hope they would be tied through their love of Mother Earth, not just through poverty and debt.

When I would talk to people, the ones who were not involved, I would notice they were really afraid that we would notice they were afraid. They were afraid that we would question them and they didn't really want to talk about it. They live in a culture of silence, and so I have compassion for them. I think that, although their voices need to be heard, they feel powerless because they are being held captive, and economically, they are. And if you disagree with eminent domain? Well, there's not a lot of Paul Seamans and John Harters [white ranchers who are allies of the tribes in the fight against Keystone XL] around who will spend the money to fight back and know they are going to be in more poverty because they fought back. It's a crazy, crazy fight when it comes down to it, but we took heart in the fact that we crossed lines that we hadn't done in a long time, coming from different ancestries. However, I think we still have a long way to go because some truths have not changed. We have to continue challenging them, but this gave us good practice and I think there are many, many issues that are going to come before us in the near future.

This all goes to our core belief that animals and plants are parts of family units that have intimate relationships with the Earth, and so we respect that. We don't have the arrogance to disrupt those relationships. We live in such a different reality than the capitalistic world. They're like children—although that's an insult to children to say that—but they are of a less mature level of thinking. It's like in recovery: you almost have to hit bottom before you can gain wisdom out of your journey. That's what I think, eventually, is going to happen. America is going to have to hit bottom in order to be able to gain this sense of respect for these intimate relationships that existed on the Earth since time immemorial.

It reminds me of a story about the mouse bean on the Missouri River. You probably have heard of mouse beans—they have to grow partially in the shade in a wet area, so when they channeled the Missouri River and they built the reservoir, it killed most of the mouse beans. We haven't been able to see any down here because they removed the trees, and so the plants had to grow out in the open and it was too hot for them to survive. But originally, the mouse beans were gathered by mice and the mice would build these little food caches. The grandmas and the mothers in our camps knew that the mice would do this, and they would go find the little caches and raid them. They would take the mouse beans because they knew that they were already picked. And so the story goes that one of the grandmas was out there and she was harvesting—she was stealing, essentially—she was stealing the mouse beans from the little mouse who had laboriously worked to create this food cache. So, the mouse looked at her and she told all the other mice, "Look at that mean, thoughtless, selfish woman.

She comes and steals our food. She has no consideration that we have babies. She has no consideration that we have to live. She has no consideration that we worked hard to get this. Look at her! She's a thief—she doesn't even care!"

And the Dakota woman who was gathering had heard their little voices (the mice hadn't realized that she could hear them) and so she stopped, and she felt really awful. Because that's exactly what she was doing. So from that day on, she talked to her people and she said, "We can't just be stealing from them. We have to be reasonable about it. If we take some of their mouse beans that they have gathered so laboriously, we have to give something in return." From that day on, they made the agreement that whenever they took—and again this goes to limited resources—they would take a little of the cache but they would give something in return to the mice. And so, that's a story of balance in the natural world and honoring the limited resources that we all share. You just don't take it all like these pipelines are doing. That's the most valuable thing for these corporate pipeline people to learn.

I think all of this organizing to protect Mother Earth, well, the Mother Earth is really doing us a favor. If it weren't for this organizing, we probably wouldn't be forced to learn how to talk to each other. You really have to look at it as an opportunity to grow as human beings. Because when we [the Cowboys and Indians Coalition] started to meet, our values were really, really different. When you deal with a dominant society that is always used to centering itself, and you must hold meetings and do business or create spaces where you're working with the Euro-American world, they usually want to run the meetings. They want to do the agenda. They want to man the resources and essentially be in charge. So we had to negotiate through that. Sometimes there was falling out and some people didn't know how to not center themselves and we had some casualties along the way. But I think the Creator put those opportunities for us to overcome. It's all about learning in the long run.

One of the main organizing challenges is negotiating through these different value systems, which are formed by the world of capitalism. I remember when we were arguing before the PUC (South Dakota Public Utility Commission), at the end when the PUC made the decision they were going to grant the permit, Chris Nelson, one of the commissioners, said something that was so patronizing it just blew me away—and he thought he was being generous! This is how different our worlds are! After he was going to vote in favor of granting the permit, he said, "You know all these months, we have been arguing and looking at evidence on why we should not grant this permit or why we should grant it—I could never figure out why Deborah White Plume all the way from Pine Ridge was so concerned about a pipeline way over here. I just couldn't get it. Now I finally understood what she said, that she cares for the land." And I thought, oh my God! I was so aghast— and he thought it was an intelligent statement!

Yeah, it made me angry and my rage came out...it was a statement of the hierarchy. "Okay, now I understand the reality that you Indians live in." I was just outraged—and he thought he was being generous. So, that's the kind of reality that we are dealing with in the fight for these sacred sites. I believe the power of prayer has to overcome this because we're fighting an intergenerational fight and it's going to take fifty years, one hundred years, to save some of these sites. We have to think of the long-term.

One of the biggest truths of colonialism is to isolate us and so, some of us, by poverty or by choice, bought into that. But in our DNA, in our language, we call We'okna: in the blood. Whether

I'm standing at the Bears Ears or I'm standing at Bear Butte or I'm standing at Thunder Butte—or wherever that memory of the land is going to mirror itself to me—I'm going to have the same feeling as somebody in Nevada or Utah because we know that it's all coming from Mother Earth. It's all coming from memories of the land, and so those lessons are thousands of years old. It is ridiculous to think that we're separate, it's totally ridiculous.

One of the kids that I work with said something to me. He said, you know how you get a worldview into the Euro-American world, the world that tries to oppress us? If you watch a movie, when you see the characters in the movie having a hard time or meeting the challenges, or whatever, they show a picture of them in the living room and they're in there all by themselves. If this was an Indian movie there would be like thirty relatives in that living room! When I watch these movies I really felt bad for them, because they are lone characters in the world—and that's the way they are conducting themselves with the environment. They have no clue, whatsoever. That's the immaturity level that they are at in regard to Mother Earth, but I'm glad that this unification across the globe is happening. I think that some of the prophecies that we were told about—that there would be water wars—[are occurring] and so our people know the instructions. They are beginning to recall the original instructions about caring for Mother Earth. The part we need to get an awful lot of work with is to educate the young as fast as we can, younger and younger. Whether that's our grandchildren or whether it's community groups, whether it's direct action groups or whether it's coalitions...we got to remember those original instructions—just not by having meetings but going out and doing those things we did in Mother Nature and interacting with those complicated families of plants and animals and whatever else lives on the Earth.

I think the keyword is "exchange," and I think in the dominant capitalistic world it's more like...taking. So again, just learning how to be a human being is probably the first tenet. These organizing efforts provide a prime opportunity to do that and I could see that happening. A lot of times the people who did come forward were the ones who were closer to Mother Earth. A lot of the farmers and the ranchers that we work with—they're out on the land all the time. They're up early in the morning and they're out there late into the night. So, they have that connection to the land. It's something we need to continue to work with, because we have that intimate relationship with the land and a lot of our young people don't have that. We really got to get with it and continue to do that. That's why I continue to work with youth.

When I grew up, my dad told me to just go adventure in the world. He said you need to go out. He said that in the old days they had a word called *ozuya*, which meant that a young person would go out and maybe get salt or maybe they'd go get the dentalium. Sometimes this would entail a journey of one or two years. When they went ozuya they didn't know if they'd come back, but when they came back they were a changed person. They had grown, they knew how to survive, they came across other peoples. When I left, I left for twenty years and lived in the Northwest—of course, I came home every summer so my kids could be at home and be able to cope with living on the reservation or with, you know, our people. I didn't ever want them to lose that contact—I wanted them as much as possible around my family. But when it was time to come home—getting older, I think your DNA tells you it's time to go home now—I could feel that pull, and so I came back. I think the thing that was the hardest to adjust was the lack of noise, because I lived in the city and I remember, at Christmas time, I was looking out the window and there was one lone person walking down the road and I thought, oh my gosh, how am

I going to handle this? The snow was falling and there was absolutely no cars, no one moving. Now I'm just used to it, but that was the biggest adjustment, was the movement, and I guess all the business of being in the city.

But once I came home, I realized that things had changed and the culture was not as strong as it used to be when I was growing up, and that created a sense of panic within me. In 1994, we had a good and wonderful experience in the Black Hills of South Dakota: myself and some other women from Ihanktonwan who are now grandmothers, we revived Brave Heart Society. We put prayers in that creek in the Black Hills. We realized that our culture was really being lessened, and that stories that we grew up with were not being told, and we panicked. We said we need help, we need to re-create a space where we can continue to do the work or the lifeway that we grew up with. So we revived Brave Heart Society in November of 1994. We are now twenty-three years of age. When we first started, we started as a women's society—just like the old society of a long time ago. *Wokadadiciye* is the way you say it in our language, and it means a special group of friends and relatives. We have raised a whole generation. When we first started, the men came to us and asked if we could start a men's society and we said, well, we can't because we're women, but, in reality, twenty-three years later, we have raised a generation of young men who have grown up around these values and around grandmothers. We try to invite as many healthy men as possible to re-create that safe feeling, in order to combat the trauma that has enveloped our communities. The greatest tool is to create a sense of safety and so we have, for the last nineteen years, we have had a community coming-of-age for girls when they reach the first method. We had 131 girls go through that ceremony and all of the girls are different. So four days that they go through are the four most important days of their life because it creates their future and their respect of not only their body, but the Mother Earth and those families of plants, animals, and all that lives on Mother Earth, and so we've been able to do that. We just had our community camp here a couple weeks ago, and we also do a hunting coming-of-age for our young men to teach them their roles. We will be doing that this fall.

We have brought back lacrosse. In our language, *thakapsica* was a peacemaking game. It's called the little brother of war and we have oral history that our Ihanktonwan Chief Wanata, which means Charger, actually resolved a village conflict by having lacrosse or *thakapsica* played. He said that once the game was over, the conflict would be left on the field, and so it was used as a tool for making peace. So now going into our sixth year, we did our sixth camp in June and we had 125 youth come from eight communities in three states and so, we've been able to revive this movement.

We also do storytelling every year. We realized that what you and I have been talking about in regard to traditional knowledge, in regard to sacred sites and these holy places that we have, the stories aren't being told like they used to be. And so we have created a space of four days in the winter when the stories are told and we invite storytellers to come to our Brave Heart lodge. We have a wonderful four days and nights of stories, delightful stories, with the snow on the ground. The origin stories, the Creation stories, the Coyote stories—of how we came to be as a people. We're making that effort to preserve that for the younger generation because a lot of the younger generation, they don't know the stories anymore.

We also have food sovereignty this year. For eleven years we had a community garden and that is an awful lot of work, so we changed the emphasis and we are building box gardens at our lodge. We have some box gardens and we're wanting to do that for the elders this coming year. And we have a harvest meal in the fall from our gardens. We average about thirty or forty families that we till gardens for. They plant it themselves, but our way is to offer the tiller.

WE FIGHT FOR THE LAND, THE EARTH, EVERYTHING: FROM BEARS EARS TO THE HIGH COUNTRY OF CALIFORNIA

CUTCHA RISLING BALDY, PH.D.

We consider all of nature to be alive, possessing both feelings and a consciousness. Hence the natural world is capable of seeing and hearing us, "blessing" us, and taking pity on us. The Earth is a physical manifestation of God's creative spirit, and we, Human Beings, are recognized by the Earth as a part of the natural world. Once I asked my one-hundred-and-eleven-year-old great-grandmother, Bessie Tripp, "Who did the old Indians say was God, Grandma?" She said, "Why, the Earth, Ever'thin'. The rocks, the leaves, the mountains.

JULIAN LANG (KARUK)

IT FEELS FITTING FOR ME THAT I WILL FINISH WRITING this article today, July 8, 2016, which marks 164 years since Congress voted against ratifying the treaties that were negotiated with California Indian tribes in 1852 and would have guaranteed tribes 7,488,000 acres or 7.5% of the state.[1] Between March 19, 1851, and January 7, 1852, three government commissioners, Redick McKee, Geo W. Barbour, and O.M. Wozencraft had met with numerous California Indian tribes and established eighteen treaties.[2] These

[1] Rawls, James J. *Indians of California: The changing image.* University of Oklahoma Press, 1986.

[2] Secrest, William B. *When the great spirit died: The destruction of the California Indians, 1850-1860.* Quill Driver Books, 2003.

treaties were supposed to result in a peaceful transfer of lands from California Indians to the United States. They were also supposed to quell the many uprisings of Native people who were fighting against a systematic genocide being perpetrated by the California citizenry.

California Indian peoples contended with what scholar Sherburne Cook called "three waves of destruction." He identified these as the Spanish Missions, the Mexican-American War/ Rancho system, and the Gold Rush.[3] For Southern and Central California, the mission system was designed as a way of seizing lands in the name of the church and converting Indians to Catholicism through the enslavement of Indian peoples. By the end of the mission period, many California Indian peoples had died, moved inland or in some cases south to Mexico, or were living in the missions without claim or ownership of any land.

In Northern California, contact with settlers was relatively late in the 1800s and mostly happened during the Gold Rush. After that, Northern California became what Hupa scholar Jack Norton calls a "deranged frontier" where Native peoples were hunted, killed at random, and their ways of life desecrated.[4] I grew up in Humboldt County, the site of a number of egregious acts of genocide perpetrated against my own peoples. Fifty-six massacres of Native people took place in the Humboldt region from 1850-1864.[5] Stories of miners and settlers (or, as Jack Norton calls them, "invaders") in Humboldt County included indiscriminate killing, rape, kidnapping, enslavement of Indian children, burning homes and

---

3 Cook, Sherburne Friend. *The Population of the California Indians*, 1769-1970. University of California Press, 1976.

4 Norton, Jack. *Genocide in Northwestern California: When our worlds cried*. Indian Historian Press, 1979.

5 Platt, Tony. *Grave Matters: Excavating California's Buried Past*. Berkeley: Heyday, 2011.

food supplies, and sliding whole villages off the sides of mountains into the canyons.

Among this thirst for gold and riches was the thirst for our land, what the settlers called a "resource." Gold would prove less profitable than expected. As a result, according to historian Brendan Lindsay, many of the Euro-American invaders "began an assault on Indigenous populations in order to wrest the land itself from their control. Land and its productive capacity would be California's new gold—indeed, in the long term, its real gold."[6]

What happened in California, and to many Native people throughout the western hemisphere, was genocide. These depraved acts of violence were not only against people, animals and cultures, but against the land. The depravity of miners during the Gold Rush in my own homeland of Northern California is often classified as human rights atrocities, but it was also built on atrocities against the land, flora, and fauna, the continued abuse of a land that many Native people in California say is woven into the DNA of the people. The old stories say we are made of the earth. The earth is like us, living. We are responsible for the earth. The earth is responsible for us. It is not just that land is sacred, it is that land protects, provides and nurtures us, so it is imperative that we do the same. Why wouldn't we? Why wouldn't we want this earth to thrive?

We sometimes hear about Indian people selling land for beads and blankets. Tall tales spread by historians that Indian people were more like children who did not know the value of the place they called home. But these stories were told mainly to diminish our claims to the land. We sometimes think the agreements, things like treaties, were just about protecting or securing rights

---

6 Lindsay, Brendan C. *Murder State: California's Native American Genocide, 1846-1873.* U of Nebraska Press, 2012.

for the people. And that was part of it. We were protecting ourselves, but we were also protecting our land. If miners can come in and build dams with no concern about what this does to the wildlife, build lakes with no concern about what this means for the trees, blow up mountains and watch the earth itself run red, spill toxins into the water and watch the fish die, then who will protect the land from this destruction? Our treaties weren't just about us, they were about the land, the earth, everything.[7]

This is where I begin in order to express the deep-seated ties that Native people have to sacred sites, national monuments or "wilderness" territories and national parks. Currently, the Bears Ears Inter-Tribal Coalition is proposing a presidentially declared national monument designation under the Antiquities Act of 1906 to protect 1.9 million acres of land in Southern Utah. They are also proposing a collaborative management strategy, between tribes and federal agencies, for the area. The coalition has already rejected one proposal by representatives from Utah because it did not adequately involve tribes in the continued management and decision-making for the area. In fact, the draft of the proposed "Public Lands Initiative" prioritized resource development and mining over land protection.[8]

Sound familiar? It does to me. Having grown up with the old stories of the Gold Rush, I am still amazed at how the rhetoric continues, the thirst for riches and resources. The continued exploitation of our land is unrelenting. And we, still unwilling to sell out our land for beads and trinkets, still fighting and resisting, still finding ways to negotiate a federal government

---

7 I draw this phrase and the quote at the beginning of this essay from *Ararapikva: Creation Stories of the People* by Julian Lang, a Karuk scholar.

8 Burr, Thomas. "Bears Ears Book will be Sent to Members of Congress." The Salt Lake Tribune, June 23, 2016.

system, we still think beyond this generation or the next generation, we still think for seven generations. If Congress can come in and strip minerals with no concern about what this does to the wildlife, drill with no concern about what this means for soil, blow up mountains and watch the earth itself run red, spill toxins into the water and watch the rivers die, then who will protect the land from this destruction? These negotiations aren't just about us, they are about the land, the earth, everything.

This is a continuing fight, a continued enactment of "bio-cultural sovereignty," where the history is written on the landscape and human memory can be so pointedly short. I have written about bio-cultural sovereignty before.[9] Bio-cultural sovereignty is drawn from the work of Stefano Varese in his book *Witness to Sovereignty: Essays on the Indigenous Movement in Latin America* and his discussion on the related issues of "indigenous knowledge and biodiversity" and "bio-cultural and socio-political sovereignty."[10] Varese asks his readers to consider:

> ...how could the indigenous outlast the European military invasion, the massive biological warfare, the systematic ecological imperialism and the meticulous destructuring of their institutions, and still initiate almost immediately a process of cultural and sociopolitical recuperation that allowed for their continuous and increasing presence in the social and biological history of the continent?

We have always maintained an active presence, knowledge, and interaction with the land, not just the sacred places, but the land

---

9 Baldy, Cutcha Risling. "Why we gather: traditional gathering in native Northwest California and the future of bio-cultural sovereignty." *Ecological Processes* 2, no. 1 (2013): 1.

10 Varese, Stefano, and Alberto Chirif. *Witness to Sovereignty: Essays on the Indian Movement in Latin America.* No. 117. Iwgia, 2006.

that sustained us in our everyday lives. Tribes have enacted and continue to enact bio-cultural sovereignty, which solidifies their relationship with the land. And we do this despite the erasure of our presence from the land by government agencies, policies, history books, and researchers. The Bears Ears Coalition writes of the land in Southern Utah:

The Bears Ears land is a unique cultural place where we visit and practice our traditional religions for the purpose of attaining or resuming health for ourselves, human communities, and our natural world as an interconnected and inextricable whole.

When we speak about health, we are not only talking about an individual, we are talking about one's health in relation to others around us and that of the land. We are talking about healing.

Our relationship and visits to Bears Ears are essential for this process. Ruining the integrity of these lands forever compromises our ability to heal. The traditional knowledge related to Bears Ears is important and irreplaceable in itself. The continuity of indigenous traditional medicine is in peril, as long as lands like the Bears Ears are not protected.[11]

And I know the importance of what the Bears Ears Inter-Tribal Coalition continues to fight for: written recognition and commitment to a co-management of the area. This is a continued refusal to be erased from the land. It is a smart move, especially in light of the federal government's history with Native land cases. In my own tribal area, we are constantly reminded of our hard-fought

---

[11] "Proposal Overview." Bears Ears InterTribal Coalition. N.p., n.d. Web. 01 Dec. 2016.

protection of sacred lands by the presence of a paved road that reaches just up into the mountains in a place that we call the "high country." The Gasquet-Orleans Road (or the G-O Road) was the centerpiece of the 1988 Supreme Court case Lyng v. Northwest Indian Cemetery Protective Association. In this case, the US Forest Service had proposed building a road that would run through the Six Rivers National Forest in northern California from Gasquet to Orleans to benefit the logging industry.[12] Local tribes protested the completion of the road, arguing that it would destroy sacred sites and in effect destroy the practice of their religions.

In my 2013 article on this case, I wrote about how tribal consultation was used as a way to dismiss Native concerns for the area:

In 1979, the Forest Service commissioned a report while planning the building of the G-O Road in which they did consult with local Indian tribes. The report, Cultural Resources of the Chimney Rock Section, Gasquet-Orleans Road, Six Rivers National Forest, stated that the road would have harmful effects on the religious practices of the tribes and that because there was no way to mitigate these issues, the road should not be built (Theodoratus et al. 1979). However, this consultation was actually used as a way to move forward with the building of the road, with the Forest Service maintaining that they had consulted with Indian tribes, but that did not mean they had to listen to any recommendations. Though tribes in the area were steadfastly against the building of the road, the Forest Service went ahead and paved a portion of the high country.[13]

---

12 Miller, Robert J. "Correcting Supreme Court 'Errors': American Indian Response to Lyng v. Northwest Indian Cemetery Protective Association." *Environmental Law Review* 20 (1990): 1037.

13 Risling Baldy, 2013.

The case was brought before the United States Supreme Court where the court overturned a lower court injunction against the building of the road, saying that while the building of the road could have devastating effects on traditional religious practices, "whatever rights the Indians may have to the use of the area, however, those rights do not divest the Government of its right to use what is, after all, its land."[14]

Justice Sandra Day O'Connor further expressed that "no disrespect for these practices is implied when one notes that such beliefs could easily require de facto beneficial ownership of some rather spacious tracts of public property."[15]

With these remarks, Justice O'Connor was attempting to further solidify "rightful ownership" by the federal government over lands in the United States. While the Lyng case had been framed as a fight for the First Amendment and freedom of religion, the concerns of the government over ownership and rights to land once again trumped the rights of Native peoples.

The land was ultimately protected against development because Congress passed the Smith River National Recreation Area Act (1990) which "added the twelve-hundred-foot G-O Road corridor into the protected Siskiyou Wilderness."[16] This action highlighted that protection of the land as "wilderness" meant designating the land as unexplored, "virgin" territory, instead of a sacred, well-managed place of inter-tribal importance. My previous article discusses some of the more tenuous language in the act:

---

14 *Lyng v. Northwest Indian Cemetery Protective Assn.*, 485 U.S. 439, 108 S. Ct. 1319, 99 L. Ed. 2d 534 (1988).

15 Ibid.

16 Echo-Hawk, Walter R. *In the courts of the conqueror: The 10 Worst Indian Law Cases Ever Decided.* Fulcrum Pub., 2010.

What is particularly interesting about the language of the act itself is that while Sec. 460(b)(b)(b)-3 allows for management of the Siskiyou Wilderness pursuant to the provisions of the Wilderness Act (16 U.S.C. 1131 et seq) it does not speak to nor specifically allow Native-based management of, interaction with, or continued use of the area. The Act does specifically mention several acceptable uses of the area including recreation, public access (including vehicular roads for recreational activities such as camping, hiking, hunting and fishing), permitted use of off-road vehicles, and permitted programmed timber harvest.[17]

Written policies have been used as an attempt to divest Native peoples of their interest in the land and also as a means to erase Native interactions with the landscape. The Bears Ears Inter-Tribal Coalition's insistence on a written legislation that protects Native interests and solidifies a relationship between Native peoples and other agencies for a continued stewardship over land areas is admirable and imperative. There are several successful contemporary examples of Native tribes and organizations working together in tribal conservation. Native American Studies Professor Beth Rose Middleton Manning explores many of these co-management coalitions in her book *Trust in the Land.*[18] Her case studies demonstrate innovations in land conservation and how tribes are working with conservation easements and land trusts to continue to steward land in a meaningful way. There has also been written scholarship on what Kristen Carpenter and Angela Riley conceptualize as Indigenous cultural property rights dictating that "certain lands, resources, and expressions are entitled to legal protection as cultural property because they are integral to

---

17 Risling Baldy, 2013.

18 Manning, Beth Rose Middleton. *Trust in the land: New Directions in Tribal Conservation.* University of Arizona Press, 2011.

group identity and cultural survival of indigenous peoples."[19] These rights should be thought of as "stewardship" rather than ownership.

The Bears Ears National Monument proposal demonstrates an ongoing fight for Native lands, a fight that is not only about Native sovereignty and investment in land conservation, but a fight that illustrates how we must live with our Earth in order to thrive for future generations. The necessity of being a voice for the earth is built into our epistemologies and ways of life. We do it for the future of all people but also for the future of our land, flora, and fauna. If governments, companies, miners, and settlers can come in and strip the land of minerals, drill with no concern, dam the rivers, siphon the water and let the land run dry, blow up mountains and watch the earth itself run red, spill toxins into the water and watch the rivers die, then who will protect the land from this destruction? We will. Our coalitions, our organizations, our scholars, our speakers, our activists, our elders. These fights aren't just about us, they are about the land, the earth, everything.

---

19 Carpenter, Kristen A., Sonia K. Katyal, and Angela R. Riley. "In defense of property." *The Yale Law Journal* (2009): 1022-1125.

SACRED IS SACRED

WAYLAND GRAY

Sacred is Sacred our ways from
the creator: our prayers our dances our songs
since the beginning of time we never surrender, our spirits are strong,
don't ask us what makes it sacred
believe our people believe the creator
our answer will always be Sacred is Sacred
remember the ancestors their spirits are strong.

BEARS EARS AND HICKORY GROUND ARE SACRED LANDS to our people, a place where our Ancestors worshipped and were buried. To seek protection for our sacred lands we must fight Big Money and call on the Government to intervene. We must face that some of our own people don't want our sacred sites protected. Ocevpofv, Hickory Ground Tribal Town of the Muscogee (Creek) Nation supports the Bears Ears Inter-Tribal Coalition in its efforts to preserve the sacred and spiritual lands of the Ancestors.

Hickory Ground has already been desecrated and developed by a small group called the Poarch Band, who stayed behind during the Trail of Tears and fought alongside Andrew Jackson to remove our people from our homeland. The Poarch were allowed to stay and given land as a reward for their betrayal. In 1985, the Poarch Band were recognized by the federal government to be an Indian tribe. They received a federal preservation grant to purchase ancestral ceremonial ground, known as Hickory Ground, in our homelands in Wetumpka, Alabama. The Poarch Band promised never to desecrate or develop Hickory Ground, but, in the end, they dug up our ancestors and built a casino resort on top of their graves. The Poarch Band claim they reburied our Ancestors in a mass grave behind their casino.

We are fighting to restore our sacred land back to nature, the way it was before the Poarch Band desecrated it. Now, at Bears Ears, Native Nations have a chance to protect the land before it is desecrated. When it comes to protecting our sacred places, we must never surrender this fight because every defeat would make it easier for the sacred lands of other Native Nations to become desecrated. We must come together as one. Tribal Nations must support each other today because it could be your Ancestors tomorrow.

The US Federal Government doesn't understand our ways or

understand what sacred means. For Native people, sacred is our natural way of life, like our breath or our heartbeat. You cannot explain or teach what is inside of us as Native people. The US Federal Government would never allow the Arlington Cemetery to be excavated, but federal laws do not protect us when Native land and burial grounds are desecrated. It seems you cannot dig up the graves of any race of people except those of the Indigenous People of this land. A person who robs the grave of a non-Indian would be committing a crime and would face shame in the media and be disgraced. But when our Indigenous Ancestors are desecrated, archaeologists get a Ph.D. and an award.

Our people have been treated like foreigners in our homeland since Christopher Columbus drifted to shore. They committed genocide, occupying our lands and removing many tribes at gunpoint from the land of our Ancestors and sacred lands. Meanwhile, American presidents stand up and make public apologies for what was done to our people over the centuries, about the price Native people paid to make this country "great." Yet we still face the same government doing the same things today—from stealing our sacred lands to making us live in Third World conditions on reservations with polluted water, diseases, black mold, and no access to adequate health care. Our youth know this and are consumed by despair. Native youth face teen suicide rates many times higher than the national average, and life expectancies on many reservations are deplorable.

There are many sacred lands under attack right now, from Bears Ears to Hickory Ground, Oak Flats, San Francisco Peaks, South Mountain, Mauna Kea, Mount Gram, the Grand Canyon and many more. In most cases, our culturally significant places are at risk due to corporate interests such as development and mining. The sometimes vast amounts of money involved make the fight more difficult to win because Greed stops at nothing. The Desecrators make campaign donations in Washington, D.C. to accomplish their crimes.

As tribes, we must unite and fight every battle as one. Natives need to remember what makes us different. This is our homeland, our sacred lands, our ways. Remember the importance of these things and forget about the man-made laws, policies and the politics. Represent our Ancestors, our ways of life, with respect and be an example to the next generation.

Sacred is Sacred. Our connections to our ceremonial and burial grounds and sacred places make us who we are as Native people. As Native people, we must stand united and support each other to protect all of the sacred places of our nations. From Hickory Ground to the sacred Bears Ears, we will fight to protect our human rights and religious freedom. We must never surrender.

THE BEARS EARS CONNECTION

MARTIE SIMMONS

We had an obligation to protect our dead.
That is why we always came home.

JOANN JONES,
former president of the Ho-Chunk Nation,
Save the Mounds Rally, Madison, WI

I AM A DESCENDANT OF THE MOUND BUILDERS, pre-contact Indigenous people, who created memorials to remember their loved ones and used them for religious and ceremonial purposes. The beautiful shapes of raised earth represented animals, people, and sacred beings. Over the course of several hundred years, these shapes, these sacred entities of vast beauty, have been destroyed in droves. Once-beautiful sacred memorials have now paved the way for streets, parking lots, universities, and shopping malls. The continued destruction of Indigenous sacred sites has affected us all: when one tribe loses their history, we all lose. To this day, it's a matter of Land Grab Roulette, no different from broken treaties, and a gamble for whose tribe will be next.

As citizens of the Ho-Chunk Nation, we serve the mounds of Wisconsin as their protectors. These are links to our past, a time before settlers entered our lives and desecrated our culture. We are deeply rooted with the land; this is where we came to be known as "The People of the Big Voice." Our history, our stories, our children are born of this land. They provide the richness and diversity of

159

my state, the meaning of hope, the meaning of love; these are not things that money could ever buy.

Our heritage and push for proper representation within the realms of our state is similar to the five tribes' connection to Bears Ears and their fight to preserve it in all its majestic beauty. To us, these places represent more than grass, hills, mountains, and trees. Our connection to them is strong; they hold the links to our past and our future. This is a place where we feel most at home to practice our sacred beliefs and to pass them on to the next generation. This cannot be done in a concrete building far from our ancestral connection; the land needs to be available for all to continue our way of life. The Ho-Chunk Nation fought their removal and always returned to protect their dead; that is still our duty as a people. We understand the vital need to be where we are most at home, where our food, our culture, and our language originated.

In 2011, President Obama reiterated promises made on the campaign trail at the Tribal Nations Conference:

> I promised a true government-to-government relationship—a relationship that recognizes our sometimes painful history, a relationship that respects the unique heritage of Native Americans and that includes you in the dream that we all share....(W)e said that even as we include Indian tribes in the broader promise of America, we're going to keep Native traditions alive.

Native traditions include sacred ceremonies on our sacred lands. These ideologies are more than superficial links, they are a part of our way of life, one that was forbidden to practice until 1978. Less than forty years ago, we fought to continue our sacred way of life.

Each tribe fought for their own practices, the capability to pass them along to their children, and to continue them as our world changed drastically around us. We cannot forget these promises of compromise; they are a lasting legacy that has changed the way many Native Americans view the government. We have forged a bond with President Obama; he has listened, learned, and implemented change. For the sake of cementing a lasting legacy, I beg you to understand what land truly means to Native Americans. While we are rich in diversity, universally we share a deep respect for our ancestral homes.

Because of the resilience of my ancestors, I now have the capability to pass on stories, history, language, and culture to my children. I can show my children the land that their ancestors fought for and some even died to preserve. This is where they belong; this is where they will always have a home. At the end of the day, isn't that where we all want to be?

Close your eyes for a moment; where can you find your tranquility? It's the place where you are completely at peace, where your soul sings and the energy of your surroundings reverberates through your body. The past and the present merge into one, the memories tied to the land are coursing through your veins. It's a heartbeat, similar to the sound of the drum; these are what make us whole, what drives our psyche. Basic biology lost in the awakening, we are not a singular being but part of a whole dynamic molecular system that is driven on bonds, we are bonded to land, and it fulfills vital needs of our existence. There is more than meets the eye, in its vast beauty, there is connection, and a truly grounding experience that provides the tools of survival. This place is simply called home.

AFTERWORD

JACQUELINE KEELER

I write this just a week after President Obama issued the proclamation on December 28, 2016, setting aside 1.35 million acres for the Bears Ears National Monument and an additional 300,000 acres for Gold Butte National Monument in Nevada. After much celebration in Indian Country, we now find ourselves facing in a just a few weeks, the inauguration of President Trump. Trump, coupled with a hostile, Republican-dominated Congress, presents a formidable challenge to the Bears Ears Inter-Tribal Coalition's vision for collaborative and congenial management of public lands that hold so much meaning—both cultural and personal—to our people.

And we are right to worry. Just five days after the President's announcement, newly re-elected Utah Attorney General Sean Reyes announced to the press at his swearing-in he would be suing the federal government over the designation.

So, we continue to read the tea leaves and look forward to maintaining the pressure on Congress over the next four years to ensure the monument is protected. And despite the proclamation, the question raised by the monument proposal—and by the writers in this book—is still before us, not yet fully decided. The question being where is the value of the land? Is it purely in the economic gain derived from it (and the further question of who benefits from that economic gain) or in the relationship we as humans (and our ancestors and other life forms) have with the land, itself?

Not to be ignored, the issue of climate change hangs over all of these questions regarding appropriate land use as well. Opposition to the Dakota Access Pipeline, alluded to in my interview "Creating a Roadmap of Reverence" with my relative, Yankton Dakota elder Faith Spotted Eagle, has gained unheard of inter-tribal support. Hundreds of tribes and thousands of allies have been "standing with Standing Rock" to help that tribe defend its right to drinking water and the right to preserve cultural sites. Yet, despite the good news of the U.S. Army Corps' denial of the easement of that pipeline, we still do not know if we (Indigenous nations) and our allies have won yet. Native America remains on the edge of its seat wondering which way the ax will fall over our lands, our people, our culture, our world.

CONTRIBUTORS

DR. CUTCHA RISLING BALDY (Hupa, Karuk, Yurok) is currently an Assistant Professor of American Indian Studies at San Diego State University. Her research is focused on American Indian Studies, gender and decolonization. She has published in the Ecological Processes Journal, the Wicazo Sa Review, and Decolonization: Indigeneity, Education and Society. She is the author of a popular blog that explores issues of social justice, history and California Indian politics and culture. www.cutcharislingbaldy.com/blog

LYLE BALENQUAH (Hopi) is a member of the Greasewood clan from the Village of Bacavi. He has Bachelor's and Master's degrees in Anthropology from Northern Arizona University. For over fifteen years he has worked throughout the American Southwest as an archaeologist documenting ancestral Hopi settlements and lifeways. He also works as a hiking and river guide, combining his professional training with personal insights about his ancestral history to provide a unique forum of public education.

KLEE BENALLY is a Diné (Navajo) traditional dancer, anarchist, musician, and filmmaker. Originally from Black Mesa, Klee currently lives in Flagstaff, Arizona, and works at the front lines in struggles to protect Indigenous sacred lands such as the San Francisco Peaks. He is the national coordinator for Clean Up The Mines!, a campaign to clean up abandoned uranium mines throughout the United States.

KIMBALL BIGHORSE is Turtle Clan, Cayuga Nation, and was born for the Yucca-Fruit-Strung-Out-In-A-Line Clan, Navajo Nation. He received a Bachelor of Science in Symbolic Systems from Stanford University and has worked in software engineering for several

Internet startups. He currently works as a web developer at the Legal Information Institute at Cornell Law School on Cayuga Nation territory, where he resides with his wife and two small children.

ALASTAIR LEE BITSOI (Navajo) is a freelance writer from Naschitti, New Mexico. He worked as a reporter for the Navajo Times from 2011 to 2015, and is pursuing a graduate degree in public health from New York University's College of Global Public Health.

ANDREW CURLEY (Diné) is a postdoctoral fellow in the Department of Geography at the University of North Carolina at Chapel Hill. His work is focused on indigenous sovereignty, political ecology, coal and development. Curley formerly worked as Deputy Director at the Diné Policy Institute at Diné College in the Navajo Nation where he contributed to projects related to tribal governance and reform.

HEID E. ERDRICH is an Ojubwe poet, writer, and filmmaker. She is a faculty mentor for Augsburg College Low-residency MFA. Erdrich also serves as the Interim Gallery Director for All My Relations Arts. She is author of five books, most recently *Cell Traffic* (poetry) and *Original Local: Indigenous Foods, Stories, and Recipes from the Upper Midwest*, which was a City Pages Top Ten food book for 2014. She lives in the Twin Cities.

MORNING STAR GALI, a member of the Ajumawi band of Pit River located in Northeastern California, is a Leading Edge Fellow focusing on the disproportionate impact of the criminal and juvenile justice systems on Native Americans. She has worked as the Tribal Historic Preservation Officer for the Pit River Tribe, and with several Indigenous-led grassroots organizations in the Bay Area. She continues to lead large-scale actions while helping organize Native cultural, spiritual, scholarly, and political gatherings throughout California. Since 2008 she has been a host on KPFA's "Bay Native Circle" and is the proud mother of four children.

WAYLAND GRAY (Deer Clan Mvskoke (Creek)) is an Ocevpofv Warrior, Hickory Ground Tribal Town, in eastern Oklahoma. He is an Activist and Protector of Sacred Places, Ceremonies, Ancestors, Burial Grounds and the Rights of Indigenous Peoples. While seeking access to the sacred Hickory Ground in ancestral homelands in Alabama, he was arrested and jailed by the Poarch Band, which had desecrated this ceremonial and historical ground by building a casino/resort on top of it and by digging up Ancestors and taking their funerary objects. An Alabama jury rebuffed the desecrators, acquitted Gray of trespassing and all other charges and upheld the American Indian Religious Freedom Act, which guarantees access to Native traditional sacred places.

WILLIE GRAYEYES is chairman of Utah Diné Bikéyah and lives on Navajo Mountain. A former Navajo tribal councilman, he was appointed to the BLM Utah Resource Advisory Council by the US Interior Department in 2015.

JACQUELINE KEELER is a Navajo/Yankton Dakota Sioux writer living in Portland, Oregon. She has been published in Salon.com, *Earth Island Journal* and *The Nation*. Keeler co-founded Eradicating Offensive Native Mascotry, which seeks to end the use of racial groups as mascots. She is finishing a collection of essays called *Not Your Disappearing Indian* and is a contributor to *Red Rock Stories: Three Generation of Writers Speak on Behalf of Utah's Public Lands*.

LLOYD L. LEE is a citizen of the Navajo Nation. He is Kinyaa'anii (Towering House), born for Tł'ááshchí'í (Red Bottom). His maternal grandfather's clan is 'Áshįįhnii (Salt) and his paternal grandfather's clan is Tábąąhá (Water's Edge). He is currently an Associate Professor of Native American Studies at the University of New Mexico and is the author of *Diné Masculinities: Conceptualizations and Reflections* (2013) and edited *Diné Perspectives: Reclaiming and Revitalizing Navajo Thought* (2014). His research focuses on American Indian identity, masculinities, leadership, philosophies, and community building.

REGINA LOPEZ-WHITESKUNK is the former head councilwoman of Ute Mountain Ute Tribe and a member of the Bears Ears Inter-Tribal Coalition. She lives in Towaoc, Colorado.

MARTIE SIMMONS is a citizen of the Ho-Chunk Nation, a veteran, and a certified HR professional. She holds a Bachelor's in Business Administration, and is a mother of two. She currently resides in El Paso, Texas.

FAITH SPOTTED EAGLE is a 66-year old grandmother who lives on Ihanktonwan Dakota Territory (Yankton Sioux) in Southeastern South Dakota. She is a fluent speaker of the Dakota Language and a member of the Ihanktonwan, although she descends from the Sicangu, Hunpati, Hunkpapa, and Mdewakantonwan and has French/Irish blood through her grandmother Julia Deloria and John McBride. She has two children.

LUCI TAPAHONSO is Poet Laureate of the Navajo Nation. Born on the Navajo reservation in Shiprock, New Mexico, to Eugene Tapahonso Sr. (Tódich'íinii or Bitterwater Clan) and Lucille Deschenne Tapahonso (Áshįįhí or Saltwater Clan), she was raised in a traditional way along with 11 siblings. The author of several poetry collections, Tapahonso has taught creative writing at universities and at the Institute of American Indian Arts.

ELIZABETH WOODY is a Navajo-Warm Springs-Wasco-Yakama artist, author, and educator. She has published three books of poetry as well as short fiction and essays. In 1990 she received the American Book Award and in 1994 the discretionary William Stafford Award for Poetry from the Pacific Northwest Booksellers Association. She is Oregon's Poet Laureate.

JONAH YELLOWMAN, a Navajo spiritual adviser at Utah Diné Bikéyah who lives on Navajo lands south of Cedar Mesa, says the Bears Ears region offers spiritual refuge as well as material sustenance for tribes.

TORREY HOUSE PRESS
VOICES FOR THE LAND

The economy is a wholly owned subsidiary of the environment, not the other way around.

SENATOR GAYLORD NELSON
founder of Earth Day

Torrey House Press is an independent nonprofit publisher promoting environmental conservation through literature. We believe that culture is changed through conversation and that lively, contemporary literature is the cutting edge of social change. We strive to identify exceptional writers, nurture their work, and engage the widest possible audience; to publish diverse voices with transformative stories that illuminate important facets of our ever-changing planet; to develop literary resources for the conservation movement, educating and entertaining readers, inspiring action.

Visit **www.torreyhouse.org** for reading group discussion guides, author interviews, and more.